The
FABULOUS

372·21

Dedications

This book is dedicated to our grandson Jack who has suffered from Chrohn's disease for the past nine years. He continues to surmount his pain and suffering with great dignity and resilience and remains an ongoing inspiration to us all.

It has been written to support greater understanding of the underpinning themes, principles and commitments of effective provision and practice in the EYFS.

All profits from this book will be donated to Chrohn's Research to support further research into a much-needed cure for Chrohn's Disease. If you are interested in finding out more about Chrohn's Disease, information is available through the following website (www. nacc.org.uk) or address: National Association for Colitis and Chrohn's Disease (NACC) 4, Beaumont House, Sutton Road, St. Alban's, Herts, AL1 5HH.

Terry Gould, November 2010

Crohn's disease affects over 100,000 people in Britain, with about 5,000 new cases reported every year. It causes inflammation of the intestine and symptoms include chronic diarrhoea, abdominal pain, weight loss and extreme tiredness, and. For a number of years I have been involved in research into the causes of Chrohn's Disease resulting in the discovery that the MAP bug is present in the vast majority of Crohn's sufferers. MAP infection is widespread in animals, including domestic livestock, and is passed to humans in cow's milk. The MAP bug has a low level of infectivity and is tolerated by the vast majority of people with no ill effects.

My research team used a state-of-the-art DNA test as well as advanced cultures to detect the MAP bug and an unexpected finding of the research showed that patients suffering with Irritable Bowel Syndrome (IBS) were also infected with the MAP bug. I have been greatly supported by the charity Action Research to develop a modern anti-MAP vaccine to treat Crohn's disease sufferers. This vaccine stimulates the immune system, so that-MAP infected Crohn's sufferers can fight the MAP bugs themselves. This vaccine is now at the clinical trial stage which will cost over £650,000 to complete

I am delighted that all the money raised from the sale of this book is being donated to support the development of an anti-MAP vaccine. I would like to take this opportunity to thank all those who have been involved in bringing this book forward to publication and to all who have purchased copies. I am sure that you will find this book a very useful read and you will, by your purchase, be helping to improve the life chances of many thousands of Crohn's Disease sufferers.

Professor John Herman Taylor, November 2010

The
FABULOUS

EARLY YEARS FOUNDATION STAGE

Edited by Terry Gould

Thanks are extended to Alison Adamus, Denise Ellis, Sheron Kantor, Julie Leach, Linda Mort, Pat Robinson and Caroline White who have each so freely and generously given of their valuable time and knowledge to add important chapters to this book.

Terry Gould is kindly donating any royalties he receives on the sales of this book to Crohn's disease research.

Published 2011 by A&C Black Publishers Limited
36 Soho Square, London W1D 3QY
www.acblack.com

ISBN 978-1-4081-4069-7

Contributors: Alison Adamus, Denise Ellis, Terry Gould, Sheron Kantor, Julie Leach, Linda Mort, Pat Robinson, Dr Caroline White
Editor: Terry Gould
Designer: Bob Vickers

A CIP record for this publication is available from the British Library.

Printed in Great Britain by Martins the Printers, Berwick upon Tweed

This book is produced using paper that is made from wood grown in managed, sustainable forests. It is natural, renewable and recyclable. The logging and manufacturing processes conform to the environmental regulations of the country of origin.

To see our full range of titles
visit www.acblack.com

Contents

Foreword

This interesting and eclectic collection of writings sets up a range of challenges and potential discussions about the Early Years Foundation Stage (EYFS) and its effective implementation.

Editing supports the flow of thinking of the reader and further enables the text to be useful to a wide range of professionals and students alike.

The fact that all profits are to be donated to Chrohn's research is more than an additional reason to purchase a copy of this interesting book which is being used to raise awareness not only of issues surrounding effective implementation of the EYFS but also of finding a cure for Chrohn's Disease.

I commend this book as an interesting, thought-provoking and useful tool to support all those connected with early years' provision.

/

Professor Lesley Abbott
(Professor of Early Childhood Education, Institute of Education,
Manchester Metropolitan University)

Preface

Having worked successfully in the early years, and delivered a great number of training courses to early years practitioners I have come to realise that for many practitioners the last ten years have been, and continue to be, a time of change, uncertainty, and sometimes confusion. Over the past three years alone there have been a plethora of new initiatives and seemingly many more are planned; often without apparent due consideration to the practitioners who have to take these on board and deliver them effectively.

I have heard more times than I care to remember, practitioners saying that they wished there was 'just one book' that they could use to help them with the key, basic aspects of their role. I doubt whether this 'one book' will ever be written but hopefully this book will go someway to providing the support and guidance that is clearly needed.

The Fabulous Early Years Foundation Stage is based on my own and colleagues' experiences as practitioners working in schools and children's centres and as advisory teachers/consultants, working with a variety of settings including schools, private day nurseries and children's centres. It is reflective of my personal belief that there are five key aspects of early years education that I term 'pillars' that underpin and hold up effective, quality and successful practice with young children. These are:

1. **A quality, enabling, learning environment – indoors and outdoors**
2. **Observation, recording and assessment**
3. **Planning**
4. **Learning and teaching**
5. **Partnership with parents**

Much has happened since the introduction of the 'Desirable Learning Outcomes' in 1998 followed by the 'Early Learning Goals' in 1999/2000 and the introduction of the *Birth to Three Matters* framework in 2003. However, although the key underpinning principles of effective provision have changed little, they do need to be understood more.

Very young children are still (as they always have been) active, interactive, dynamic and hungry learners. They need to be presented with learning opportunities that are exciting, meaningful and which satisfy their individual needs and styles of learning.

Nothing I have seen over the years has changed my firm conviction that effective early education must start from what the child already knows and can do. This is again the key to effective implementation of the Early Years Foundation Stage (EYFS), which became statutory from September 2008.

Terry Gould
November 2010

About the contributors

Alison Adamus

Alison was born in Addis Ababa, Ethiopia and lived there until the age of four when she moved to Northern Ireland. She later completed a PGCE at St Martin's College, Lancaster, specialising in Early Years. Alison has extensive early years teaching experience as a Foundation Stage advisory teacher in Blackburn with Darwen, later moving to her current role of early years advisory teacher, working in schools, children's centres, and the private, voluntary and independent sector. She has provided support, training and workshops, both locally and nationally.

Denise Ellis

Denise Ellis is a retired educational consultant. During her long career she worked as a primary school teacher predominantly within the Foundation Stage but also within Key Stage 1 and Key Stage 2. She has worked for Hertfordshire, Humberside, Cheshire and Manchester local authorities, taking on roles which have included class teacher, SENCO, Foundation Stage co-ordinator, deputy and acting head, often within challenging inner city areas.

As a consultant for Manchester LA she supported a range of settings as they developed their EYFS provision and has delivered a range of training. She continues her work as a school governor at a local primary school and is currently working as a freelance consultant.

Terry Gould

Terry has contributed to a range of books, magazines, journals and training videos on the early years and worked as a consultant for a number of local authorities, private training providers and computer software publishing houses. Part of his work has involved advising architects, planners and schools on the design and development of outdoor grounds. He has led the writing of a wide range of early years guidance materials for practitioners. He regularly writes articles on early literacy for publications, such as English 4-11 published by the English Association. Terry has been a teacher representative on the Early Years Development Group at the Manchester Metropolitan University where he has contributed to conferences, seminars and workshops. He is an assessor for the Early Years Professional Award and is an experienced moderator for the Early Years Foundation Stage Profile. He recently worked for Manchester City Council as an EYFS consultant and a learning strategy officer. A regular speaker at conferences, he now works through 'The Early Years Consultancy' offering a range of training courses and consultancy across the Midlands and the North West of England.

Sheron Kantor

Sheron trained as an early years teacher and has since worked in a range of settings and roles with children, parents, teachers, and other early childhood educators. She has contributed to the writing and development of curriculum guidance materials/ frameworks and led development projects for several local authorities. Sheron's research and development work in the area of 'parents as partners' has its roots in her experiences as an EYFS consultant and family literacy project manager, and is inspired by her recently completed MA in Early Childhood Education. She is currently a learning strategy officer with Manchester City Council and is widely respected for her training and consultancy work with early years practitioners across the North West.

Julie Leach

Julie trained as an early years educator in the 1980s and began her career at an infants' school in Oldham. This school was an innovative place whose philosophy put children right at the centre of everything. Having started as a probationer, she left the school in 2003 as deputy headteacher, to fulfil a lifelong ambition to work for Manchester City Council Education Partnership as a Foundation Stage consultant. There followed four and a half years working with a truly remarkable team of people who really did change the face of early years in Manchester. In April 2008 Julie left Manchester to join Stockport LA as an EYFS consultant where she continues to apply the philosophy of putting the child at the centre and heart of everything she does.

Linda Mort

Linda has extensive experience of teaching children in the EYFS and Key Stage 1. She is the author of 20 books on early years education and regularly contributes to leading educational magazines. She jointly established and ran for 13 years an independent nursery school in which she is still actively involved. She is now an early years consultant and educational director of a children's media company which has won many awards.

Pat Robinson

Pat trained at Manchester Metropolitan University between 1988 and 1992, majoring in Religious Studies and Special Needs. She worked in Cheshire, teaching reception, Year 1 and Year 3/Year 4 classes before moving to work in Manchester in 1998. This was initially in a reception class and then as a nursery teacher and foundation stage co-coordinator in a primary school where 30 per cent of the children had some level of special educational needs (SEN). She later became a lead practitioner for Manchester whilst assistant headteacher at the same school. She has further trained for SEN work and has a particular interest in autism. She joined the Manchester local authority team as a SEN Foundation Stage consultant in 2005 and has recently been promoted to the role of learning strategy officer.

Dr Caroline White

Caroline is a consultant clinical psychologist and Head of the Children and Parents' Service (CAPS). She is based at Booth Hall Children's Hospital, Manchester where she leads and manages the citywide, multi-agency CAPS early intervention service. Caroline is also an accredited 'Incredible Years' (IY) trainer and over the past ten years has delivered many talks to IY parent groups in community settings and trained hundreds of professionals in accredited IY parent training workshops worldwide. She has successfully contributed to the development of Manchester's multi-agency parenting strategy and consults nationally and internationally on parenting matters. A regular speaker at conferences, her research interests and publications include service development and cognitive aspects of parent training.

Introduction –
Implications for good practice

A short introduction to the EYFS

Terry Gould

The EYFS guidance is a framework comprised of the following:

- Principles into Practice cards
- *Statutory Framework*
- *Practice Guidance*
- CD-ROM of additional resources and information
- Large poster of four themes, principles and 16 commitments.

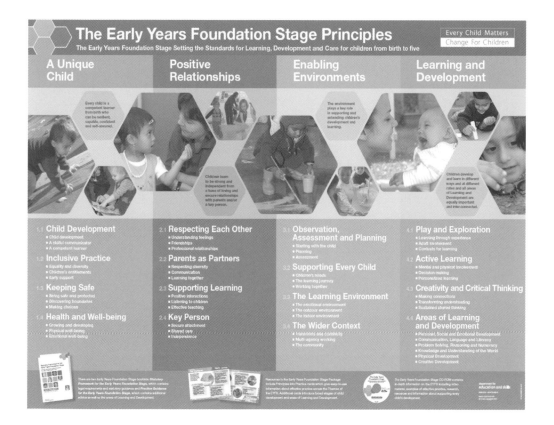

Each of the four themes:

- The Unique Child
- Positive Relationships
- Enabling Environments
- Learning and Development

has an underpinning principle which is supported by four commitments. These are focused on through a set of A4 colour-coded cards – matching those of the poster – that should be used by staff teams to further develop their practice and provision leading to improved outcomes for children.

The CD-ROM accompanying the pack provides more detailed guidance on aspects of the EYFS, such as 'key person', 'learning environments' etc. and is a must in order to engage fully with its supporting contents.

The *Practice Guidance* covers some key aspects of meeting the requirements in the statutory framework in the following areas:

- meeting diverse needs
- partnership working
- flexible provision
- play
- quality improvement
- transition and continuity
- learning and development requirements
- safeguarding and promoting children's welfare
- staffing arrangements including ratios.

It aims to ensure that from birth, the best start in life becomes a real and accessible entitlement for every child. This is in recognition of the impact such a positive start will have on the future life chances of all children and their families.

The *Statutory Framework* has been introduced through the Childcare Act 2006 and sets out the background and legal basis for the EYFS and its underpinning principles. As well as giving details of the learning and development requirements it also sets out the new welfare requirements for all settings. It amalgamates the good practice from the *Birth to Three Matters* guidance, the *National Standards for under 8s day-care and childminding*, and the *Curriculum Guidance for the Foundation Stage* into a new framework that strongly focuses on high quality provision which supports exploratory play and active learning. In this it builds on, among other things, the research from the EPPE project (2003) which supports the key, effective role of play in children's learning and development.

> 'Play underpins the delivery of all the EYFS; children must have opportunities to play indoors and outdoors.' *(EYFS 2007)*

Key aspects of the EYFS are:

- Its basis is a principled play-based approach.
- It covers from birth to the end of the Foundation Stage (Reception year).
- It provides guidance for an integrated approach to care and education.
- It strengthens the previous links between *Birth to Three Matters* and the Foundation Stage.
- It incorporates elements of the National Standards.
- It supports and ensures a consistent approach to care, learning and development from birth to the end of the Foundation Stage.
- It supports practitioners' planning, care and learning that is right for each child at each stage of their development.
- It is about 'stages' rather than 'ages' of individual children.
- It has four overarching themes: The Unique Child, Positive Relationships, Learning and Development and Enabling Environments – each with a key Principle and four Commitments.

The role of the adult in provision is a key element within the EYFS framework. Overall, the adult role is identified as requiring a number of key skills and attributes which include the ability to:

- sensitively observe and respond to children
- plan the next steps in their learning and development
- reflect objectively on their own practice and the provision offered
- work effectively with parents and carers for the benefit of the child, the four EYFS themes and their principles and the 16 commitments
- provide the role of key person and use this to advocate for children
- implement the four EYFS themes.

There are four critical aspects that support learning and development and which need to be enabled and facilitated by practitioners within the EYFS and which are embedded in the themes, principles and commitments.

These are:

- **Quality Care** – ensuring that positive relationships, based on love and care, impact on development and provide a secure base upon which to build for the present and the future;
- **Quality Interactions** – where adults sensitively engage in the learning process so as to influence and challenge children's thinking skills and processes through involvement in open-ended questioning and sustained shared thinking;
- **Quality Enabling Environments** – providing well organised space and stimulating resources including displays that are enabling for all aspects of children's interests and needs – indoors and outdoors;

- **Quality Experiences** – stimulating engagement and interactions with resources utilising their preferred learning styles indoors and outdoors. These must be relevant, real and fun for the child, as well as providing equality of access for all to learning that is meaningful; within a context that provides every child with appropriate space and time to support their active involvement.

Prior to the EYFS provision and practice, a great deal of language/terminology was used which sometimes led to confusion and uncertainty. The EYFS provides an opportunity to reflect on this and to remedy the situation as well as guidance on the overall practice and provision within settings. All of this will support a shared exploration of understanding and meaning so that we as practitioners can focus on our work with children with clarity and direction.

The Children Act 2006 places duties on local authorities to be 'market managers' of childcare within their localities and ensure that parents/carers are provided with high quality, affordable provision and information across all childcare services.

KEEP (Key Elements of Effective Practice) is strongly reflected within the Principles into Practice cards and the *Practice Guidance*, which advise that through initial and ongoing training and development, practitioners need to develop, demonstrate and continuously improve their:

- relationships with both children and adults;
- understanding of the individual and diverse ways that children learn and develop;
- knowledge and understanding to actively support and extend children's learning in and across all areas and aspects of learning;
- practice in meeting all children's needs, learning styles and interests;
- work with parents, carers and the wider community;
- work with other professionals within and beyond the setting.

Planning in the EYFS

Planning should be based on the principle that children learn most effectively when they are motivated and interested by the activities in which they engage. Ongoing regular observations of children's interests, needs and learning styles should be used to plan activities that stimulate, challenge and inspire. As planning is often a key concern among many practitioners this aspect will be dealt with in more detail in a later chapter (Chapter 6).

There are a number of key messages we should consider in all aspects of our work with young children and these are that **the EYFS…**

- is for every child
- principles are the starting point for effective practice
- builds on what practitioners already do well
- brings learning and welfare requirements together
- supports continuity and coherence for all children
- offers a renewed range of opportunities for all children to realise their entitlement to the very best start in their lives through improved practice and provision from practitioners.

We do not provide for our children in the UK in isolation, and the EYFS framework and guidance has been influenced and informed by the work of some of the great educators of recent times, and the best of educational and care provision from around the world.

In this first chapter Julie Leach reflects on the EYFS through its four themes in the context of her study tour visit to Reggio Emilia.

Inspiring experiences

Reflections on the EYFS through a visit to Reggio Emilia

Julie Leach

'We don't talk about preparing children for the future; it is the present that is important. We do not know what the future holds. Childhood is the best time of life, it should be enjoyed.' *Carla Rinaldi*

In May 2005 I was privileged to spend a study week in Reggio Emilia, Northern Italy, as part of a delegation from Manchester City Council Children's Services. This inspiring week consisted of visits to pre-schools and infant-toddler centres as well as lectures from educators, pedagogical 'atelieristias' and consultants from Reggio Emilia. There was also time to discuss our experiences and thinking within our own group and with other participants. On our return there was a period of reflection and a response to our visit that was shared with the practitioners of Manchester.

Three years later I am still thinking about my participation in the study week. It has had a profound effect on my own philosophy and I often think about the many vibrant and moving experiences with which I was privileged to engage. I have been reflecting on the Reggio Emilia approach to early years education in light of the EYFS which became statutory in England in September 2008 and through this chapter will share some of my thinking by exploring the four key themes of the EYFS:

- A Unique Child
- Positive Relationships
- Enabling Environments
- Learning and Development.

I shall show how these can be related within the context of the experiences of my Reggio Emilia study visit.

▶ Key Theme: A UNIQUE CHILD

A focus on the commitment areas of 'Child Development' (card 1.1) and 'Health and Well-being' (card 1.4).

In the EYFS there is a commitment to the principle of 'a competent learner'. This was a key element from the *Birth to Three Matters* framework. But what do we understand by the term 'competent learner'? Babies are ready to learn as soon as they enter the world, from other people around them and from the world they are living in and this continues as the young child grows and develops. In Reggio Emilia this is a key part of their philosophy of children and education – children are born as citizens of the city. Each child is seen as a unique citizen with rights, with interests and with ideas. Children are citizens of the present and not the future.

Carla Rinaldi, during one of her lectures as part of the Study week, stated very clearly that each educator has '*the responsibility of knowing that every child is unique.*' In Reggio Emilia, childhood is seen as a unique time and not a preparation for other parts of their life. Sometimes there is a feeling in our own culture that we are rushing children through childhood to get them to the next stage. Again, Carla Rinaldi summed up this idea in the following way, '*we don't talk about preparing children for the future; it is the present that is important. We do not know what the future holds. Childhood is the best time of life, it should be enjoyed.*'

On the 'Child Development' card 1.1 we are posed the following challenge: 'How to meet the differing and competing needs of every child, while being 'fair' about time spent with individual children.' In Reggio they recognise the individual within the group, never forgetting that each individual, unique child has their own 'story' which needs to be listened to.

The emotional well-being of each child has been given a high priority in the EYFS alongside physical well-being and growing and developing. The EYFS materials give practitioners ideas of how to promote and develop each individual child's emotional well-being. There are a number of tools which practitioners can use to 'measure' this including the 'Leuvan Scale of Well-Being and Involvement'. This is a tool which practitioners can use to monitor how their provision and practice is promoting the emotional well-being and involvement of the children in their care.

In Reggio Emilia, the concept of developing a child's emotional well-being is not measured or monitored. This is because it is recognised as an intrinsic part of everything that they do. The way that children are true partners in their own learning and are so totally involved in the decision-making ensures their emotional well-being. Unlike in the U.K. they do not see the young child as vulnerable but rather as capable. In Reggio Emilia I am sure that they would not necessarily understand the phrase 'low self-esteem'. This is in part due to the culture of Italy in general and the region in particular but this ethos of everyone having a say, playing their part and having responsibilities is also part of the philosophy of each centre. Loris Malaguzzi wrote a poem which epitomises the Reggio Emilia view of the child. It is called 'The Hundred Languages of Children'. (See Editor's notes on page 28).

Key challenges for The Unique Child theme within EYFS provision, posed by the Reggio visit:

- How can we support our children's emotional well-being more effectively by ensuring it is an intrinsic part of everyday provision?

- How can we support children developing a much greater partnership in their own learning, so that this is done *with* them rather than *to* them?

- How can we make learning more effectively personalised so that every child's needs are met and interests are fostered?

Key Theme: POSITIVE RELATIONSHIPS

A focus on the commitment areas of 'Respecting Each Other' (card 2.1) and 'Parents as Partners' (card 2.2).

The EYFS aims to promote respect by ensuring that each individual is valued and that differences are appreciated. In Reggio Emilia this is seen as paramount to the work of the centres. The pre-schools and infant-toddler centres were created out of conflict arising from the devastation of the Second World War. The city respects all its citizens and the centres are part of the city. There was a definite sense of equality between children and educators within each of the centres. Education is a shared process. It is not being done to one set of individuals by another set of individuals. The emphasis at Reggio is that learning is a group process although the individual within the group is recognised. This sense of working and learning within a group requires respect for each other's ideas, interests and space. Debate and discussion is used as a way to solve problems and negotiate meaning. Educators arbitrate during arguments and disagreements but the children are encouraged to negotiate and come to a group solution/decision.

In our English system this level of mutual respect is not always as easy to achieve and this is acknowledged within the 'challenges and dilemmas' section of card 2.1.

A key phrase which is heard time and again, both with Reggio itself and in any documentation about Reggio, is that children and their educators are *'co-constructors and co-researchers in learning'*. During one of the lectures an educator said: *'We need to stand beside the children, not in front – give value to their thoughts, ideas and theories.'* All educators and other staff involved with the centres are valued highly and their opinions sought. There is a sense of 'solidarity' between all those involved including the children and their families. There is substantial time given up to reflection and sharing of ideas and thoughts.

'**Parents are a child's first and most enduring educators.**' This phrase was heard and read during the trip to Reggio and it is now written boldly on commitment card 2.2 within the EYFS. However, I think that we do have some way to go to ensure that this is actually seen as effective in practice as it is in the Reggio Emilia centres. In Reggio the parents are seen as full partners and co-constructors alongside their children and educators. Parents are encouraged to fully contribute to the developments of the projects. There is a true respect for a parent's knowledge about their child and the role that they can play in their child's education.

A key phrase which was truly seen in practice was '**Reciprocity and Participation**'. Educators, children, parents and community all give, receive and learn. Parents are involved in the decision making process within each centre. There is a very flat structure of management in the centres with all involved having equal say and equal right to be involved. Parents can be as involved as they want to be. In the U.K system this is something that we sometimes use as an excuse for poor parental engagement. But do we really engage with all parents in ways that work for them and in a way which shows that we do respect their views and ideas? In Reggio the children's life outside school is genuinely valued and links between school and home positively encouraged.

The parents' noticeboards in the Reggio centres were working tools which changed and evolved each day in response to children's projects and the dialogue with parents. Each centre's noticeboard was unique to that centre reflecting the interests, ideas and thoughts of the children, their families and educators. There was no sense of 'corporate values' but of complete ownership by that centre's community.

During my visit to Reggio I witnessed genuine time to talk to parents at the beginning and the end of the day. On one occasion I witnessed a dialogue between a pedagogista, educator and parent about a child's learning that day. The dialogue was rich in a way that truly engaged the parent in her own child's learning. They talked as equals and I felt that the educators learnt as much, if not more, from the dialogue than the parent. The home is apparent within the centres. For example there were soft toys on the beds, items from home in trays and home linked resources were being used to develop projects in school.

Parents have total commitment to the centres. Many parents contribute during the Study week and become volunteers after their children have left the centres. In

England we believe strongly in parental involvement but are we truly committed to full parental engagement?

Key challenges posed from the Reggio visit for the Positive Relationship theme within EYFS provision in England:

- How can we develop a 'truer' partnership between all staff where all contributions are seen of equal worth within a framework where many are on very different terms of pay and conditions?

- How can we create a truly genuine partnership and engage with our parents/carers in ways which value parents' contributions as at least of equal value to those of practitioners?

- How can our settings/provision provide a greater reflection and valuing of the home environment?

Key Theme: ENABLING ENVIRONMENTS

A focus on the commitment areas of 'Observation, Assessment and Planning' (card 3.1) and 'The Wider Context' (card 3.4).

The EYFS states that each child must be seen as an individual with a unique set of abilities and that all planning must start by observing each child. In this way practitioners can understand and consider each child's current interests, development and learning. The Reggio Emilia centres embrace this philosophy wholeheartedly. Themes and topics flow with the child. There are no predetermined topics/themes which are identified by the adults. Instead a number of *projettzione* may be ongoing at any one time. *Projettzione* develop from children's interests and ideas. They may last for a day, a couple of days, a week or longer. They may be revisited and could last for many months. Some of these projects involve one child, a group of children or the whole centre. The parents and the whole community are often involved. The projects are documented thoughtfully and thoroughly and the learning is made visible throughout the centre and, at times, beyond. Planning is flexible and belongs to the children as much as the adults. There are daily gathering times at the start of each day once all children have arrived. The rooms are designed to allow this with seating areas to create a forum space. This gathering time allows children to talk about their current interests and ideas and to plan the projects with their friends and educators. These gathering times can be quite volatile and noisy as all the individuals put forward their ideas. There are sometimes disagreements and the educators act to facilitate problem solving. As projects are planned and decided in this way by the whole school community there are few written plans. However, the educators in Reggio put their time and efforts into documenting the learning that is taking place rather than planning potential learning in advance. Educators are 'looking, listening and noting' throughout the session, alongside interacting, facilitating, teaching and learning with the children. Educators have time to really listen to the children. Listening is a key part of the philosophy. Time is given to the educators to analyse their observations and share them with their colleagues. Documentation is written up daily to share with the parents/carers and for the children to see their own learning and as a point of reference for them. There is a sense of the immediate visibility of the learning. The challenges and dilemmas written within the EYFS card 3.1 cover a number of these elements.

EYFS states that true partnership, working across the whole community, will support children's development and progress towards the *Every Child Matters* outcomes. This can be a challenge. In Reggio Emilia I was immediately struck by the sense of community within the city and the fact that the centres were seen as integral to this community. Education of children is the responsibility of the whole community. Community and school are intrinsically linked and work reciprocally with each other. Many projects take place within the city and the city asks the children to become involved in civic projects. One of the most famous of these was when the city asked one of the centres to become involved in designing a theatre curtain for one of the municipal theatres within the city. There is a true sense of belonging to your family, your school and your community. This was obvious throughout the visit both within the centres and around the city. The design of the buildings and the arrangement of the furniture and resources are planned very carefully. They are designed to reflect the city itself as well as aspects of Italian culture. In all the pre-schools and infant/toddler centres children go out into the community regularly to have 'encounters' with the city beyond the confines of their building. The pride that the city has in its young children, their families and their educators is apparent for all to see. The children were truly viewed as citizens with much to contribute not only in the future but today. Children are listened to not only by their parents and their educators but also by the community and the city.

Key challenges the visit poses for the Enabling Environments theme within EYFS provision:

- How can our learning environments and provision be developed to reflect that they are a key part of the local community?
- How are we able to ensure that our planning, observations and assessment systems and processes reflect the *Every Child Matters* agenda?
- How can we ensure that we find the time to listen to children so that their ideas and interests and experiences leading to their learning are documented to reflect the child's voice?

Key Theme: LEARNING AND DEVELOPMENT

A focus on the commitment areas of 'Play and Exploration' (card 4.1) and 'Creativity and Critical Thinking' (card 4.3).

The EYFS commitment to developing play and exploration states that children's play should reflect their wide ranging and varied interests and preoccupations. The commitment to developing children's creativity and critical thinking allows children to discover connections. Supportive adults should encourage children to think critically and ask questions. The practice of the Reggio Emilia centres has a great deal to teach us about both of these areas.

During the study week we heard a pre-school educator describe the way that they work together:

'A right to have time, give time to each other, to discuss, to explore.

A right for making explicit, shape and time are intrinsic.

A time for dreaming, knowing, imagining.'

This philosophy means that there is time to develop a deep and rich learning. Children can work on projects for long periods of time – over several days or weeks. There is a culture of allowing children's 'work in progress' to be kept so that it can be further developed at other times. The child is recognised as a researcher. Creativity is nurtured by the space, resources and interactions. In the centres, resources are used to stimulate and draw children into exploration, investigation and dialogue. Resources in all the centres are displayed beautifully and considerately, drawing you to them to touch and investigate. The quality and richness of the materials offered to the children every day is exquisite. The way that the materials are presented to the children can change their potential. In Reggio they are presented beautifully and sometimes the purpose of resources is not only functional but aesthetic. They provide flexible materials with potential for open-ended exploration; materials and resources to provoke responses, to inspire curiosity, exploration and discovery.

This use of materials was particularly evident in the ateliers (the artistic spaces in each centre) which are supported by an atelierista who works within each centre as a member of staff. The atelierista may be a painter, a sculptor, a musician, an architect or designer. The use of the atelier and interactions with the atelierista allow children to explore their own creativity and to investigate their theories.

In the Reggio centres there was a great sense of freedom to explore with no specific routine or adult-focused tasks to dominate events. Risk taking within a secure environment is a feature of each of the centres. Educators and parents feel that this develops children's confidence and allows them to challenge themselves. One of the educators put it in the following way:

'It is important for children to take risks. We create artificial situations yet life is made up of difficult situations. We need to help children face these.

Children need to encounter the world in its entirety.' This is a challenge within the U.K. system which the EYFS acknowledges.

One of the most powerful images of my time spent in the centres was of highly motivated children who were not easily distracted even when large groups of English people were watching them. Very young children could focus for very long periods of time. Another powerful memory of observing within the centres was a particular interaction between a child and educator. This allowed the child to articulate her ideas in dialogue with a truly listening educator. The child knew that she would be listened to and her ideas valued. This was truly 'sustained shared thinking' in action. This is a key aspect of the EYFS 'creativity and critical thinking' commitment. In Reggio children are encouraged to analyse their own learning, understanding what they need to do next. This produces very self-confident children.

The last words I leave to Loris Malaguzzi and Carla Rinaldi whose quotes sum up the whole Reggio Emilia experience for me:

'Nothing without joy', Loris Malaguzzi

'Knowledge is a beautiful adventure to be lived everyday,' Carla Rinaldi.

Key challenges the Reggio visit poses for the Learning and Development theme within EYFS provision:

- **How can practitioners support risk taking within secure environments, allowing children to challenge themselves and through this, develop higher levels of self-confidence?**

- **How can the 'Creativity and Critical Thinking' commitment of EYFS be made a reality through enabling more sustained shared thinking to take place?**

- **How can we offer our children opportunities to engage with a wider range of rich and exciting materials and resources which provoke responses including inspiring curiosity, exploration and discovery?**

- **How can we ensure that children's creativity is truly enabled?**

▶ Editor's notes

To complement Julie's superb opening chapter to the book, I am including the inspirational poem 'The Hundred Language of Children' by Loris Malaguzzi, which gives us insight into the ethos, beliefs and values of the work of Reggio Emilia and many of the things Julie talks about in her writing. This for me is enlightening us to the amazing things that children are capable of, if we back off and give them the space and opportunity to really explore their interests. It reflects how the EYFS tells us to give children time and space and the chance to be themselves with their own ideas and to be the 'Unique Child' they were born to be.

The Hundred Languages Of Children

The child
Is made of one hundred.
The child has
A hundred languages
A hundred hands
A hundred thoughts
A hundred ways of thinking
Of playing, of speaking.
A hundred, always a hundred
ways of listening
of marvelling, of loving
a hundred joys
for singing and understanding
a hundred worlds
to discover
a hundred worlds
to invent
a hundred worlds
to dream.
The child has
a hundred languages
(and a hundred hundred hundred more)
but they steal ninety-nine.
The school and the culture
separate the head from the body.
They tell the child:
to think without hands
to do without head
to listen and not to speak
to understand without joy
to love and to marvel
only at Easter and at Christmas.
They tell the child:
to discover the world already there
and of the hundred
they steal ninety-nine.
They tell the child:
that work and play
reality and fantasy
science and imagination
sky and earth
reason and dream
are things

that do not belong together.
And thus they tell the child
that the hundred is not there.
The child says:

No way. The hundred is there.

Loris Malaguzzi

Bibliography and further reading

Pope Edwards, Carolyn and Forman, George E. (1993) *The Hundred Languages of Children: Reggio Emilia Approach to Early Childhood Education.* Ablex Publishing Corporation.
Abbott, Lesley and Nutbrown, Cathy (2001) *Experiencing Reggio Emilia: Implications for Pre-school Provision.* Open University Press.

Websites

zerosei.comune.re.it/inter/reggiochildren.htm
www.sightlines-initiative.com

We're human too ⟨2⟩

The role of the EYFS advisory teacher/consultant

Alison Adamus

'Local Authorities have a statutory duty to provide information, advice and training to their Early Years workforce, and Early Years consultants should be at the forefront of delivering this. They are key players in ensuring that a local authority's quality improvement strategy is implemented in all settings in a way that impacts on the lives of children and their families, offering measured support in inverse proportion to success.'
(*DCFS 2008: The EYFS Consultant's Handbook*)

▸ A day in the life of an advisory teacher (or 'Oh, I'd love your job!')

'Oh, I'd love your job! What do you need in order to become an advisory teacher?'

I smiled at the slim figure of Jilly looking at me. A non-committal sort of smile, with every intention of avoiding actually answering the question, or of appearing rude, of course! My mind darted between thoughts of exactly what skills you do need to become an advisory teacher and thoughts of precisely why the slim figure before me would never make one. I guess that's one skill you need to acquire…the ability to give a non-committal smile.

My day had started with its usual transition from mother – cook, cleaner, bank manager of two demanding teenagers, to advisory teacher, desperately trying to be professional. 'Mum, have you ironed my black jeans?' echoed from the bathroom. Gritting my teeth, I replied quite simply, 'No'. Having spent two hours the previous evening steaming everything in sight, convinced that half the items had not been worn since the last ironing session, I decided that the question did not deserve more than a single word reply! 'Mum, I need money. When will you be home? What's for my lunch? Have you seen my…' It has got to the point where I can predict some of the questions and be prepared in advance.

Once in the car, with sandwiches placed by my side and briefcase, fully loaded, in the passenger footwell, I realised that, yet again, I was 15 minutes later than intended, and so was bound to get caught up in the traffic as each car desperately jostled for its place to join the motorway.

The car practically drove itself down the usual route and on each corner I could hear the wisssh thud of plastic boxes in the boot as they slid and crashed into the side of the vehicle. Knowing how full the boxes were, I dreaded opening the boot and finding the scattered papers of records, handouts, course materials, phone messages, formats and endless 'to do' lists shuffled like a deck of cards and then promptly dropped with a lack of skill never seen in Vegas. The opening of the boot always depressed me. The initial impression is that of being disorganised, untidy and lazy which, in fact, I am not. I desperately wanted it to display the effort, willingness to take things home, the hectic multi-tasking...but it never did!

Checking my diary at the next red traffic light, I knew that I would make my appointment on time. I usually did! Good time keeping is a must for an advisory teacher. My first visit was to a small nursery. I had been a week earlier and made some suggestions on improving writing opportunities in their domestic role-play area. I officially signed in and was greeted by the manager. Then came the more difficult bit… to be welcomed into the role-play by the children! After several minutes of observation and discussion with the manager, I felt a tug on my trouser leg. 'Hey you,' came a confident, but small voice. 'You doin' them letters now?'

Clearly I was at a disadvantage, but made the most of the verbal engagement, which led me to understand that my red coat clearly indicated that I was a postal worker and that I needed to be 'Doin' them letters now' AND getting the recipient (three years old) to sign for them. Mission accomplished – to improve writing opportunities in the domestic role-play area. 'Great, a special delivery for me at number eleventeen.' Mmm… next mission, to use some number names accurately in play.

The remainder of that visit involved advice about course attendance and an agreement to revisit with regard to resources. On departure, I was required to sign and log the time. A boy asked me what I was doing. Having been informed that I was logging the time, he danced away calling out that I was sticking without glue. Logging – sticking…Ah well! I laughed. Another skill that's much needed.

By the time I reached my next appointment, my mind had refocused (another skill), yet again, on the agenda of the meeting. Having done what was requested of me from the previous meeting, I rehearsed my presentation in my head, feeling satisfied that I would come across as efficient and knowledgeable. Within seconds of the opening of the meeting however, this was altered as the agenda changed. I was requested to take minutes and feed back on two additional agenda items. (Being flexible, adaptable and able to take minutes – just a few additional skills). I accomplished this without letting myself down and stayed behind to decipher and rewrite the minutes, while still fresh in my head. Adding the typing up to my 'to do' list, under update calendar, resource work and additional work that had unfolded during the meeting.

Glancing at my watch as I slumped into the car again, I mentally plotted my route to get to the other side of town. The first visit of the day and meeting were now firmly logged in the back of my mind, while I adjusted my thoughts concerning the next visit, a large nursery with several recent changes in staff, including management. Needing a whole new team-building approach, developing relationships, trust, vision etc and all instantly – mmm I wonder what skills that would involve. To be friendly, decisive, positive, focused, sensitive, imaginative, professional, clear, organised, realistic… I could go on, though I'm sure they don't all appear on an advisory teacher's job description.

The afternoon went well – self-evaluation skill, being able to answer many enquiries – knowledgeable, make some suggestions – observational, creative, and clearly made a good impression as I was genuinely thanked on departure for enabling the team to feel so positive.

While bundling my overloaded brief case into the car I heard yet another small voice call out to me. 'You sticky passport for plane?' A wide grin greeted me from a small boy. One hand firmly held in his mother's and the other clutching bits of paper, with ribbons streaming and strategically placed pom poms. Under his arm was clasped a long cardboard creation.

A few days earlier I had been 'inspected' by passport control and duly been refused permission to board the plane (a neatly arranged set of chairs with sticky note numbers precisely stuck on the back of each) and quite rightly too. After all, I had no passport! Seeing my dilemma and after some clever observation and excellent negotiation skills, he was able to take my borough's identification badge, complete with the necessary photograph and 'stamp' it with a red sticker. This clearly provided me with a 'sticky passport for plane' and I had several adventures to Blackpool, Pakistan, and my uncle's home!

I glanced down at my badge, delighted to see that the red sticker was still attached. I held it out for the passport control officer, his mum looked on rather confused. 'Good' he said, 'Where you want to go?'

'Well, where are you going today?' I enquired. 'Home', came the reply. 'Then I'd like to go home too, if I may. Which is the best way?' 'You pilot and fly that plane.' He held out his arm, dropped his cardboard creation and pointed in the direction of my car.

My journey home as a pilot was filled with delight as I recalled the first time I had met Adam. He had only just arrived in the country, spoke hardly any English, and to see how he had developed made me feel quite honoured to be working with some of the most wonderful small people in the world. Not a bad job, this advisory teacher role!

Just one more call to make. To get some visit records signed on the way home. Just a quick drop-in. Not expected to be the most enjoyable drop-in. A setting that struggled with understanding the most basic concepts meant by words like quality, commitment, Early Years etc. A setting that had more input than most from the team, and yet was still deemed to be only satisfactory by Ofsted. Progression through an action plan was painfully slow, if indeed in the right direction at all.

I had the report and pen to hand ready to get it signed and retreat. Not that I was being cowardly, but I had a future visit booked and once across the threshold I knew I could be there for hours. Not today, please not today. The skill to be able to say 'No.' I darted across the road, up the broken steps – still not repaired – and rang the doorbell. The slim figure of Jilly greeted me with a forced smile.

'Can't stop,' I said. 'Just need these signing, please.' I dared not ask how things were, in case she responded: 'Swanning around? Oh I'd love your job. What do you need in order to become an advisory teacher?'

I pulled up outside the supermarket. I just needed a few things before getting home. A full trolley later, I returned to the car, opened the boot, accepted the blast of 'giving the impression of being disorganised, untidy and lazy', promptly closed it and placed the goods on the back seat.

Finally parking the car on my own drive, I glanced down at the side of me. There, a familiar sight, an untouched bag of sandwiches. Ah yes that most necessary of skills – survive without nourishment during the day!

As you can deduce from this short story, which though made up but at times too true to be other than reality, is aimed at giving a somewhat humorous insight into the role of the advisory teacher. It is a satisfying job, but also at times very demanding, and at others downright difficult, and there are a wide range of skills needed to be successful in the role, not least that of diplomacy. Practitioners think that you know it all until what you advise doesn't suit them and that's the point at which it can get quite difficult.

Experienced and knowledgeable advisory teachers are a rare breed and getting even rarer in some parts of the country, as new people are being thrust into a role which takes some years to perfect and which often demands perfection from the start.

I guess those reading this chapter who will gain the most from it are those less experienced new faces to the role and those practitioners in settings who would like the inside information on us. Well, we are human and we do care about not only the children in the settings but also the adults who provide for them. All we want is to make the provision the best it can be for the children who only get one start in life.

The profile of the advisory teacher/consultant

So what are advisory teachers and where do they come from?

They are experienced teachers who are seconded by local authorities from classroom positions, usually for two or three years or employed on a permanent basis. They are usually linked to specific groups of settings and may work on specific projects, such as special educational needs, or on particular curriculum or practice areas. They are normally based in the local authority offices or a teachers' centre, and travel round to different settings. In some authorities they are also children's centre teachers for some of the time and their outreach work supports a range of linked settings. Advisory teachers are required to keep up to date with the latest educational initiatives and help settings to interpret and implement these. The implementation of the EYFS is a prime example of this.

Job titles can vary; advisers also tend to be known as consultants. Local authorities provide advisory teacher services to meet the training and development needs of practitioners in settings – including schools – to help to raise the quality of outcomes for young children in the EYFS.

They do this by, among other things:

- arranging in service training both on and off site
- helping settings to prepare for inspection by The Office for Standards in Education (Ofsted)
- undertaking post-Ofsted support for settings
- identifying and disseminating good practice.

The role of the EYFS advisory teacher/consultant

If anyone thinks the role is an easy one or that recruitment and selection is an easy process let them then reflect on the long list that one local authority required the advisory teacher to be able to do in a recently advertised job description:

> Provide professional advice, training and support to Early Years Foundation Stage practitioners so that standards of teaching and learning are raised, in accordance with the requirements of the Early Years Foundation Stage, the Early Years Foundation Stage Profile, LBR Children and Young People Plan, the 10 Year Strategy for Childcare, Every Child Matters, and the SEN Code of Practice

- lead the development of inclusive practice in early years settings including providing professional advice to specific service providers as requested by the early years pedagogy advisory team manager
- lead area SENCO support for children with SEN in private, voluntary and independent sector early years settings
- contribute to the achievement of early years and childcare service goals, and to development of the service within the Children's Trust through:
  - the building of effective working relationships with the early years and play team
  - understanding and meeting the requirements of the EYC Eligibility for 3 and 4 year old Funding Agreement
  - the requirements of the adopted quality assurance scheme
  - responding to Ofsted and the writing of action plans
  - the identification of training needs and the implementation of plans to meet them
  - promoting inclusive practice and fulfilling the duties of the area SENCO
  - contributing to the team practice support worker meetings
  - reporting to the team manager on the effectiveness of advisory support to EYFS settings and on issues that arise from advisory visits
  - contributing to the development and delivery of in-service training, in collaboration with other members of the EYFS advisory team
  - supporting practitioners in all early years settings to improve practice, including: modeling good practice to staff and management, providing workshops on-site to whole staff teams, leading off-site training and evaluating impact on provision

The Fabulous Foundation Stage

- the Key Elements of Effective Practice (KEEP):
  - report on professional development programme progress and issues arising
  - identify measures for promoting inclusive practice in EYFS settings
  - monitor and evaluate effectiveness in raising the quality of provision
  - ensure SEN/Inclusion focus is part of all EYFS teamwork
  - contribute to the development and delivery of Inclusion/SEN training to EYFS practitioners
  - maintain up-to-date databases on work undertaken
  - represent EYFS on the Pre-School Liaison Group and other organisations with an SEN focus
  - provide information to the Children's Resource Centre Head, Education lead, as requested
  - liaise with colleagues from health and social services within the Children's Trust, to inform on issues and coordinate responses
  - contribute to the development of SEN services within the Children's Trust
  - liaise with the schools' SEN advisor, the early years and play team manager, and other members of the Advisory team where relevant, to inform on SEN/Inclusion issues and coordinate appropriate responses
  - liaise with the voluntary sector and any other LA based teams and agencies working with children with additional needs, to inform on issues and coordinate appropriate responses
  - contribute regularly to the maintenance of training, advice and support databases and to the development of Children and Young People strategic plans
  - contribute to the development of transition policy and practice, to ensure children's learning progress from home to pre-school, between early years settings and phases, and from Reception to Year 1
  - respond to the EYFS regional advisor national agenda, as requested by the EYPA team manager
  - attend local network meetings and contribute to the early years newsletter
  - undertake specific projects as directed by the team leader, including working with other teams and organisations as required
  - plan and organise own time and work programme, in agreement with team manager
  - be responsible for submitting expenses, accountability and progress reports to the team manager and to attend team meetings as required
  - maintain an up to date awareness of equal opportunities issues, particularly in relation to the provision of early years services.

Having read this long list it highlights just how much is now expected from the consultant/advisory teacher within the EYFS and that it will probably take some time for anyone new to settle into the role. Fortunately, most authorities have excellent induction programmes and offer a full range of support but the fact remains that before too long, high expectations of the advisory teacher come into play. Advisory teachers grow into the role and year on year take on more and more. With them, it's about dedication and a real desire to improve outcomes for all children. So if you, like Jilly, were thinking they just 'swan around', be enlightened from now on.

The *EYFS Consultants' Handbook* (2008) successfully summarises the skills required and areas of expertise needed by advisory teachers/ consultants into five areas:

- strengthening leadership for learning and development to take place
- developing practitioners' ability to support and deliver effective learning and development opportunities
- facilitating partnership for learning and development with all those involved in the process
- supporting progress through effective learning and development
- supporting high quality environments for learning and development to take place.

It then goes on to create grids which highlight the roles and responsibilities of the EYFS consultant/advisory teacher in more detail. This is a 'must read' for all consultants/advisory teachers, both 'old and new' to the role, and for any other persons interested in this. It can be downloaded free from the National Strategies website.

If you feel you have the qualities to take on such a role then don't let anything put you off – people with such qualities are needed to support our settings. Without experienced and committed people in the role, many settings would flounder. The new EYFS offers a great new learning horizon for children but needs the right kind of professionals to support its effective impact on outcomes for children. A key part of this group of professionals is the advisory teacher/consultant.

But remember, you are human, as exemplified through the opening storyline, 'A day in the life', and never forget it even when you are rushing to make that first appointment after dropping the children off at school, having had no sleep, as one of them was ill in the night. But don't expect too much sympathy from your clients at the settings; they just need you at the top of your game there to help them get through for the benefit of their children.

▶ Editor's notes

The role of an EYFS consultant/advisory teacher is complex and needs equally complex and high levels of skills. These include most significantly:

Interpersonal and communication skills – the skills to get on with people, to communicate effectively at all levels, to be open and honest and able to deliver hard messages at times, but at all times to remain professional and caring and to value, care for and respect those we support.

Analytical and problem solving skills – the ability to be able to analyse both qualitative and quantitative data and to help settings and schools to build up their own capacity to self-evaluate, and use this data to move forward practice and outcomes for children. This will include being able to recognize any significant barriers and how these can be broken down, and solving problems they create.

Observation and intervention skills – being able to see what is needed without 'destroying' the practitioners we support and enabling them to see what we see for themselves. This means taking in all we see and making a mental note but not always pursuing every issue at once. The art of prioritisation, sensitivity and diplomacy (even when delivering hard messages!) come into this very much, as well as the skill of getting the school/setting to 'buy into the change/s' and take ownership of them, by doing things with them and not to them.

All of these require EYFS consultants/advisory teachers to sell themselves, as Alison shows she does, before they try to get the setting/schools to do anything.
This needs them to display:

PASSION
COMMITMENT
PURPOSE
PROFESSIONALISM
A BELIEF IN THE SCHOOL/SETTING
GENUINE CARE

Only then will they get the best out of those they are supporting and with whom undertaking intervention works!

Bibliography and further reading

EYFS Consultants' Handbook (2008) DCFS National Strategies.
Key Elements of Effective Practice (2005) DCFS National Strategies.
Progress Matters (2009) DCFS National Strategies.

Making it happen! 3

Developing and maintaining a quality indoor learning environment

Terry Gould

'The environment plays a key role in supporting and extending children's development and learning.' *(EYFS 2007)*

It is not by accident that this chapter appears early in the book. The learning environment is of critical importance in supporting all learning and teaching with very young children. Those fortunate enough to have visited or read about the Reggio Emilia pre-schools of northern Italy will know how strongly they value the learning environment both indoors and outdoors; so much so, that they call this 'the third teacher'. Chapter 1 by Julie Leach will have given some insight into the Reggio Emilia provision to those less familiar with it.

The quality – enabling learning environment is the first of the five pillars I have identified which underpin effective EYFS provision and practice. Without this being appropriately in place we are unable to set the foundations for independent exploration and learning through the child's senses, and much of our aspirations and efforts will consequently be ineffective.

The EYFS recognises and acknowledges the crucial importance of both the emotional and physical environment which are often inextricably linked. Practitioners should continuously reflect upon the learning and development opportunities the learning environment has to offer and its enabling impact on outcomes for all children.

Practitioners should self-evaluate on an ongoing basis both daily and over time, including reflections on how effectively the provision:

- enables children to be independent and make their own choices of materials and resources
- inspires children by provoking motivation for learning that captures their imagination and lights up their minds
- provides sufficient opportunities for children to get deeply involved in exploration, discovery, imaginative and representational play as well as problem solving activity
- enables children to engage in challenging but achievable tasks
- provides quiet places where children can think and play as well as larger open spaces for them to engage in physical activity
- allows children to take risks and make mistakes within a safe environment
- fosters social and emotional development and promotes a sense of well being
- supports every child's learning through planned and predicted experiences.

Principles and values underpinning a quality learning environment

A quality-enabling learning environment is one where space, time and materials/ resources are planned and organised to give all children the opportunity to explore, experiment and make decisions for themselves, enabling them to play and learn at their own developmental level.

To be effective, such planning and organisation needs to ensure that the learning environment:

- provides opportunities for learning to take place in a variety of situations both indoors and outdoors
- encompasses all six areas of learning through the development of a range of provision areas in which resources will be creatively and imaginatively organised and presented so as to be independently and flexibly accessed and used by children
- has appropriate interactive displays which should be created within some of these areas and enhanced on an ongoing basis in line with children's interests and identified learning needs and which should appropriately engage the interest of children
- provides areas which offer opportunities for children to engage with the resources in ways that should be meaningful to children in terms of their existing experiences including the cultural and social aspects of their community, and hence should captivate their interest
- should ensure that there are clearly designated places within the developed provision areas where children can display things they produce

- supports frequent engagement with found and natural materials and which should be continuously encouraged and supported
- has areas which are clean, well maintained and presented
- has text which should sometimes be printed or written in dual language;
- offers an appropriate balance between floor and tabletop space for activities ensuring that tables and chairs do not dominate the room, the overall principle being that each child does not need his/her own table and chair
- has an outdoor area (which will be addressed in more detail in Chapter 4), is organised with varying activities in mind and, as appropriate, zoned into areas.

Before we begin to think about developing a learning environment for young children, a key question we need to ask ourselves as practitioners is 'what is it like to be a child in the EYFS?'

So, imagining you are a child in the EYFS, here is your first task – you decide on age, gender etc.

Task 1: Discuss and then record:

- What sorts of things are in your thoughts today?
- What are you feeling today?
- What words and/or gestures will you use to express your ideas, thoughts, feelings and needs?
- What is in your pocket or bag?
- What are you interested in?
- What would you choose to eat for lunch?
- What things can you do?
- What are your favourite things?
- What places have you been to recently?

Hopefully, you will have recorded some interesting ideas.

When you have appropriately engaged with this, I have another task for you to do.

Task 2: Create a definition of a 'child-like child'

Decide on age, etc. yourself, record it on paper with a picture or diagram (or both). Then decide what you can learn and/or share with others from the two tasks and how this can be reflected and embedded in your future work with young children.

Why did I ask you to complete these 2 tasks? Well, you probably guessed right! The real purpose of these tasks was to highlight the fact that we must have a good understanding of what young children are like and how they learn and develop if we are to be able to create appropriate experiences for them – experiences which enable them to grow, learn and develop and so meet their entitlement to the very best start on their educational journey.

We need to know this before we can begin to think about the learning environment and resources they need, i.e. the provision we create for them. Remembering that experiences lead to skills and later these lead to and support understanding, so allowing a transference of these skills into other situations.

Thinking about provision

What learning experiences do you think children should have had by the end of their time in the EYFS that are really important for their learning? Create a list of these.

It might include making dens, splashing in puddles, listening to stories, making models, going to the seaside, visiting a farm, riding a pony, sharing and turn-taking, using their imagination, listening to others, building a snow person, making mud pies, digging a hole in the garden, planting and growing seeds, making friends, writing their name, climbing up trees, etc, etc.

Was it difficult or easy?

Did you have them sitting up, cross legged, with their arms folded for 20 minutes in assembly every day or being seen and not heard? Hopefully not!

Well done, because you have so far constructed images of what a young child really is like and what they want and need to engage in – in effect what the child needs for their learning and development. We need to continually revisit these key areas, with our colleagues, so that we are as a team enabled to develop deeper and richer levels of understanding of children. We must do this often so that we continually ensure that as providers of education and care we meet our children's learning and development needs in ways which stretch and challenge them, as well as making them emotionally strong and keep them feeling good about themselves.

The resources and equipment we organise and make accessible to children must offer them rich, meaningful and satisfying experiences which motivate them to want to be involved. These resources and equipment must enable children to operate and interact with them both independently and with some adult support.

Whilst we must plan for and structure children's learning opportunities we must at times ask ourselves a crucially important question:

What do we value more: children's learning or our own planning?

We must constantly be mindful of the need for children to be in control of their own learning through play and active engagement. Think of the images of the child you constructed earlier and the 'can do' aspects of these and remember that 'The more we do for children the less they do for themselves' (Maria Montessori) which leads nicely on to the key aspects of an environment which truly supports learning.

Let's now begin to think about an appropriate learning environment for the young child:

'What would an environment look like that is totally supportive of children's learning and development?'

That's a really huge question, so perhaps it needs breaking down a bit, starting by looking at things that don't help, e.g. loud bells, carpet areas that are too small, too many tables and chairs, poor access to the outdoor area, poor staffing ratios, limited access to good story books.

Now make a list of all the things you personally wouldn't want to be or to happen in your 'classroom' and then make sure they are never allowed to be there now or in the future. When you have done this you will be much more ready to move on to developing or reviewing provision areas, and so giving children all the things you believe that they do need!

Starting to develop or review provision areas indoors

The way the environment is organised and the resources/equipment provided within this (both indoors and outdoors) will very much depend on the ages/stages of development of the children. When starting to plan and develop provision areas it is necessary to have a clear idea of which ones are to be set up and where these can best be sited within the learning area as a whole.

Practitioners should individually, and as a team, carefully consider:

- the purpose of each area
- how the area will be used
- how the area will be organised
- what key resources will be provided in the area
- how the area will be included in the planning
- the role of the adult.

The following grid is an example of a format practitioners could use to review an existing area. This could easily be adapted to support a new area being developed.

Review of _____ area	Date _____	
Aspects to consider as a whole team	**Existing provision**	**Ideas for future development**
Purpose of the area		
How the area is used		
How the area is organised		
Key resources in the area		
Ways the area is included in planning		
Maintenance of the area e.g. clearing up, renewing resources, cleaning, etc.		
Role of the the adult in the area		

The areas which could be developed for toddlers up to two years of age include:

- music area
- mirrors area
- painting area
- mark-making area
- water area
- sand area
- domestic role-play area
- quiet/cushions/carpets area.

The following is a list of provision areas that are potentially appropriate to be developed, subject to space, for children aged two years+ up to five years of age:

- book area
- listening area
- investigation/Exploration area
- writing area
- creative workshop area
- water area
- sand area
- ICT area
- structured role-play area
- small world area
- construction area including blocks
- maths investigation area
- malleable area
- music area
- soft play area.

Additionally there will be a need for an appropriately sized gathering area/s.

It will always be necessary to bear in mind the stage of development of the group of children, the number of children, the space available and the children's identified interests and needs and recognising that, where space is limited, some areas can be effectively combined (e.g. small world area and construction area or music area and listening area).

Although desirable it is not necessary to have all the above workshop-type areas but an appropriate selection of these. When deciding on this the ages/stages of development of the children will be the starting point.

For smaller groups of children, e.g. in small private settings, one gathering area will be sufficient. However, for children in larger, and school settings for children aged three+, two gathering areas will need to be incorporated. Gathering areas will be used for circle/group times. Where two gathering areas are required, ideally there will be one larger and one smaller area – one being able to cater for up to 13 children and the other able to cater for the whole class of up to 26 children in a nursery class. To make the most effective use of the available space gathering areas will double up during the day as provision areas. In practical terms the book area and the construction area are very suitable provision areas to choose for this purpose, but others, too, can be utilised for this 'doubling up'.

Having decided on the areas to be developed, and being mindful of the space available, then it is a good idea to draw up a sketch outline plan of how it will all look and how each of the areas will be defined using storage, display and divider furniture. You will need to justify that you will be providing a good range of provision areas which promote learning and development opportunities appropriately, covering all six areas of learning.

Next, it is very useful to undertake a resource audit to establish what furniture, storage units and resources are already available for the project. Once this is done, then it's a matter of sourcing additional appropriate furniture, storage units and resources/equipment within your budget. The following is an example of a format which could be used to complete this type of audit.

Resource audit for _____ area   Date _____

Storage units, display surfaces and dividers		Resource storage trays, boxes, baskets etc.		Resource items	
In place	Required	In place	Required	In place	Required

Important notes:

- While waiting for any additional requirements to be sourced, it's always good to make a start on using and developing what you already have, and involving the children in this where possible. Ease of access to resources for all children will necessarily be a key consideration so that children can see the tools, resources and materials that are available for them to use, are able to select these as and when they need them, and put them away easily.
- Resources not meant to be accessible to children should be stored away from the learning environment so as not to confuse them.
- Practitioners should invest time, and patience, in training and supporting children in becoming skilled decision makers – selecting and using resources, and returning them to their appropriate place after use, as well as generally tidying up after themselves.
- It is of critical importance that practitioners do not worry unnecessarily when they observe children electing to move resources from one area to another or decide to combine different types of media (as long as this is purposeful) as this is an effective and important part of them creatively using the provision.
- The provision of familiar and new tools and resources will provide and enhance new and often different ways of thinking and problem solving within a secure background of continuity of experience and expectation.

What will each developed provision area need?

Each provision area needs appropriate definition so that it is clear to children, parents and other visitors what its purpose is, and some of the best ways it can be used.

Some things to include are:

- large signage of the area e.g. BOOK AREA
- an A4 laminated sheet outlining the PURPOSE OF THE AREA
- an A4/A3 laminated sheet with continuous provision planning for the area
- several A4 laminated photos of children using the area, with short explanations of the learning taking place. This should be in parent/carer friendly language
- an interactive display where appropriate
- a designated place where children can display things they make or sort
- resources and equipment in appropriately sized and labelled boxes, trays etc. with use made of silhouettes for resources not in boxes, e.g. music area, sand area etc.

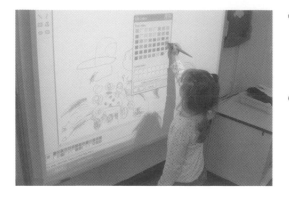

- a signing-in board where children can attempt to write their name to record they have visited the area – where appropriate to stage of development
- a sign or alternative resource indicating how many children can play in the area at any one time; possibly supported by badges or necklaces etc. on hooks – where appropriate to stage of development

Maximising the potential of learning in the developed provision areas

Each of the developed areas has the potential to support learning opportunities across all six areas of learning. However, in order to maximise this, practitioners should plan:

- to enhance the provision areas in line with children's interests and learning needs
- to promote the language development the area can support so that this language can become embedded
- for a range of intended experiences
- for the role of the adult
- how resources should be accessibly stored.

While much of the above can be achieved informally, through discussion among practitioners, it is advisable to formalise this into individual long-term continuous provision planning sheets for each area. To be effective this should cover the following:

1. key learning opportunities across the six identified areas of learning – working towards Early Learning Goals (ELGs) and linked appropriately to Development Matters
2. listed permanent resources
3. organisation of permanent resources
4. practitioner support/ interaction – including support, talk and modelling
5. intended experiences for children
6. information about how each of the four EYFS themes is supported by this area.

Storing resources

These need to be easily accessible to children and actively displayed to stimulate their interest. The aim should be for smaller well-labelled boxes to be used where appropriate and possible. For example the train set could be split into a box for the tracks, a box for the engines and carriages, a box for the play people and a box for any mini buildings and structures such as bridges, station, etc.

Storage units should facilitate displaying the resources attractively and should be varied in size, shape and height. Some should include display boards close by or attached, and others should provide places for children to display the things they have created, including models made in the construction area, drawing and writing in the writing area, and clay representational models in the malleable area. The units should also give the areas a sense of identity by the way they are arranged, so creating appropriate floor surface areas, while still ensuring they are cosy and inviting to the young child.

Boxes in which resources are stored should be appropriate for use and not overfilled. For example wicker-type baskets are great for storing small amounts of books in the book area while plastic boxes are better for storing water play area resources. It is always worth taking time to consider the type of storage units and the storage boxes used within each area.

Practitioners will find that children use the resources better when these things are taken on board at the planning and design stage of the learning environment. Often the best way is to move things around until you and the children are happy with them – a sort of trial and error way of working in some instances. Watching how the children use the resources will give great insight into how effectively and appropriately the storage and definition of the area is working and will sometimes lead to changes being made in response to this.

Editor's notes

It's important to recognise that each and every setting/school will be unique and that this will need to be reflected in the continuous planning and the nature of the provision offered. The ideal scenario is that when the child comes into the setting their eyes light up because what they see, hear and smell speaks both to them and to their parents/ carers. We need to ask ourselves one simple question: '*How would I feel if my child attended this school/setting?*' If you are in anyway unsure or downright negative then it is time to have a serious rethink of what you are offering, as it is very likely indeed that it will not be in line with the EYFS. If you have concerns about what you are offering you are probably right, so talk about these professionally with your colleagues and then try to make the improvements that would make you and your child smile if he or she was in your provision. Of course, there is a saying that 'until you can see it in your mind you cannot do it!' So do, if possible, make some visits to settings/schools where the indoor environment is considered to be of a high quality with the 'wow factor'. Take your camera and capture things you want to emulate but always remember that your setting is unique; it can never be exactly like someone else's. Also, see if you can book to go on a course or two where you know you will get the right input to help you on your journey.

Bibliography and further reading

Early Years Toolkit (2001) Salford City Council.
Early Years Foundation Stage Guidance (2008) DCFS National Strategies.
Featherstone, Sally and Bayley, Ros (2011) *Independent Learning in the Foundation Stage*. Featherstone Education.

If in doubt, let them out! 4

Developing and maintaining a quality outdoor learning environment

Terry Gould

'Whenever possible, there should be access to an outdoor play area, and this will be the expected norm for providers. In settings where outdoor play space cannot be provided, outings should be planned and taken on a daily basis, unless circumstances make this inappropriate.' *(EYFS 2007)*

'Access to the outdoors is more than a recreational exercise; it offers activities planned to develop skills and confidence across the whole curriculum.' *(Select Committee on Education Report 2001)*

We need to get the balance right and get our young children outdoors, where often they need to be, to learn and develop in a wide variety of ways. Quality outdoor learning opportunities are not an optional extra, but every child's basic entitlement. It's important that practitioners recognise that developing outdoor provision is not about simply duplicating the indoor area but about providing learning opportunities across the six areas of learning in bigger, bolder, messier and noisier ways. These should provide learning in more appropriate, more active and more meaningful ways for children than can be provided indoors.

There is a growing body of research work that clearly indicates the wide range of benefits children can gain from actively learning outdoors, including how it can inspire and enrich their learning. Prior to the EYFS the *Curriculum Guidance for The Foundation Stage* (QCA 2000) and *Birth to Three Matters* (2004) highlighted a clear expectation that children will be playing and learning both indoors and outdoors in their earliest years. The EYFS guidance (2007) clarifies the need and entitlement for daily outdoor experiences for all children and recognises that with all the current concerns around safe, independent, outdoor play within our communities, early childhood and outdoor play are sadly no longer naturally synonymous.

The outdoor learning environment offers children the opportunity to learn in different ways from the indoor environment across all areas of the curriculum. It is

imperative that every child feels included and this is the key challenge to practitioners when developing this important aspect of provision. If inclusion is the key element of outdoor provision, then we need to consider what this involves and how we can make it happen in practice.

Inclusion outdoors values diversity and starts with attitudes and understanding. When developing the outdoor provision and planning its use, it is crucial to consider the needs of all children. This will involve valuing children as individuals through consideration of the following:

- children's known interests
- children's existing skills
- children's identified needs
- children's existing knowledge

and recognising, as a whole team, that all of these can be stimulated and supported effectively through an appropriately developed and resourced 'outdoor classroom'. Margaret Edgington (2003) expresses it well: 'Outdoor Learning makes a major contribution to children's development. Young children will be missing out on important learning opportunities if quality outdoor provision is not available to them regularly.'

Once this recognition and understanding is in place and an ethos clearly established, we can effectively plan, deliver, further develop and monitor the learning opportunities we offer and their effectiveness in terms of learning outcomes for children. In this way, it is about creatively and imaginatively overcoming the

barriers that all practitioners face in some form or other in creating and maintaining quality outdoor provision. The learning and development opportunities offered to all children outdoors must be **more than just physical** and must be appropriately accessible in line with EYFS requirements. Such opportunities must be stimulating and motivating and include the provision of space for the dynamic expression of emotions, individual personality and feelings. They must extend beyond those provided in a confined indoor space through implicitly including all children by the way the 'outdoor classroom' is designed and utilised.

For example: **they should include larger scale sand and water play opportunities and access to outdoor learning in all weathers.**

The outdoor environment offers many important learning opportunities and experiences that cannot be provided indoors. Children can engage in minibeast hunts outdoors and then use information books or the Internet to find out more about the living things they find. Books on the weather and seasons, while supporting learning to some extent, can never replace that real experience of the weather and seasons which the outdoor area can provide. Yet there are still a number of EYFS practitioners, senior managers in settings and parents/carers who do not value the learning that can or does take place outdoors. Why this is so may be historical but may also be based on mistaken assumptions. The EYFS challenges such mistaken assumptions.

Why is outdoor learning so effective?

Part of its appeal includes the fact that it can offer the following:

- **more exciting and active learning**
- **materials can be combined and transformed freely**
- **a flexible and open-ended approach to the use of materials and space**
- **living things can be observed in their natural habitat**
- **the weather and seasons and the effects of nature can be experienced first hand.**

EYFS guidance clarifies the importance of outdoor learning, stating that it:

- **supports the development of a healthy and active lifestyle**
- **offers children opportunities for physical activity and movement**
- **promotes a sense of confidence and well-being**
- **provides opportunities for developing harmonious relationships with others through negotiation, turn taking and cooperation**
- **supports those children who learn best through activity and movement**
- **provides safe and supervised opportunities for children to experience new challenges, assess risk and develop the skills to manage difficult situations**
- **supports children developing creativity and problem solving skills**
- **provides rich opportunities for imagination, inventiveness and resourcefulness**
- **gives children contact with the natural world and offers them unique experiences such as direct contact with the weather and seasons**

(Effective Practice in Outdoor Learning EYFS 2007)

Resources for outdoor learning

Resources for outdoor learning are best when they are open-ended, stimulating and interesting for children. Being open-ended means they can be used in many different ways and for all sorts of purposes. Resources which enable children to construct or change their environment have great value across all six areas of learning. Large resources such as crates, hollow blocks, blankets and guttering encourage children to work and play together. The best resources, however, are adults who are enthusiastic and tuned into children – adults who support the play but don't dominate or interfere with the flow of children's own ideas and thinking. It is vitally important that the weather is utilised to support learning and is not allowed to become an inhibiting factor. Hence, resources that provide for the ever-changing weather should be a top priority. Children can then explore and investigate without feeling uncomfortable and too hot or too cold. Some of children's favourite resources for outdoors include:

- rain gear and wellies
- ropes (long and short, thick and thin)
- hosepipes
- wheelbarrows
- watering cans
- umbrellas
- blankets, sheets, ribbons and pieces of fabric including muslin sheets or net materials, shiny fabric etc.
- camping items
- large hollow blocks and planks
- pegs, string, large strong elastic bands and tape for joining things
- wooden logs
- pop-up tents
- milk and beer crates
- pipes, guttering and funnels

- brushes – brooms and decorating brushes
- boxes (range and variety)
- buckets (range and variety)
- old clothes horses – wooden ones are best
- kitchen utensils, pots and pans, sieves and colanders
- range of sizes of tyres
- pebbles, shells and other natural resources
- cardboard carpet inner tubes
- bubble pots
- camouflage nets
- bamboo canes
- jumbo chalks
- bags and baskets – including suitcases, back packs and shopping trolleys.

Many of these don't cost a great deal of money – indeed some may be obtained for minimal cost or even free!

Designing and planning an outdoor area

When designing and planning the outdoor area, practitioners should think first of the range of experiences they want the children to engage in, just as they will have perhaps already done with the indoor environment. Zones can be created outdoors which support the use of a wide range of portable and open-ended resources.

These zones should include a range of fixed equipment such as climbing frames, etc. which are particularly useful in areas where there is no, or limited, natural 'architecture' already in place. This is often the case in inner city or built-up areas.

The four zones that take up the most space are:

- **The ball and running area** – a flat, level, open space for children to enjoy unimpeded running, develop ball skills, dance, skip and enjoy space.
- **The climbing and adventure area** – an area of safer surfacing which will be designed to incorporate a range of fixed equipment and/or space where portable equipment can be used so as to offer gross motor physical development opportunities. Children will be able to experience height and to climb, swing, crawl, and balance.

- **The roadway area** – a road system allowing children the opportunity to enjoy a range of imaginary, sensory and physical activities, make decisions, find routes and engage in role-play.

- **The natural area** – an entirely natural area which offers children the opportunity to investigate, design, explore, experiment and construct. This area will enhance children's sense of adventure, make believe, fun and enjoyment, e.g. in den building.

After these, other areas which can be included and which will usually require less space are:

- **The growing area** – provision of opportunities for children to grow, care and learn about plants, vegetables and flowers. Ideally this will be situated close to a water supply (outdoor tap or water barrel).
- **The sitting, reading and gathering area** – an area where children can engage with or participate in storytelling, reading storybooks, quiet reflection, listening to taped music stories or poetry. It can additionally be used as a social gathering area.
- **The wildlife area** – this area will be clearly defined and allowed to become wild. It will be planted and resourced to attract a variety of wildlife, and where children will be enabled to observe, enjoy and learn.
- **The sensory/musical garden area** – children will be supported in experiencing a range of sensory stimulation including experimenting in making sounds using larger and different resources than indoors, and also in experiencing a range of sensory stimulation from natural and made resources, plants and materials.
- **The natural materials area** – this area will provide opportunities for large-scale experimentation, exploration and imaginative play with a range of natural materials including sand, water, large pebbles, different-sized logs, large shells, pine cones etc.
- **The creative/sculpting area** – this area will provide resources, equipment and materials which support a range of opportunities for children to work on a larger scale and in messier ways than is possible indoors. This will include painting, drawing, sculpting and making models.

- **The imaginative area** – although children will play imaginatively in all outdoor areas, this area will be dedicated to imaginative play in its own right. As such it will offer children a range of opportunities to engage in purposeful, larger scale role play and construction using a wide range of materials and resources.

- **The digging area** – this will provide children with the opportunity to dig using a range of tools and to explore natural materials including soils, stones etc. and living things such as worms and other minibeasts.
- **The performing arts area** – this will provide children with opportunities to express themselves through drama and singing.

Having all these areas will depend upon the space available and the age/stage of development of the children and, clearly, areas with limited space will have to be developed in more limited ways and will be unable to offer all of these.

All of the above areas will need to be supported with a range of portable and open-ended resources, as well as collections and outdoor resource boxes (sometimes on an outdoor resource trolley). They will need an ongoing maintenance programme including daily visual safety checks.

By having a developed zoned environment, with some fixed items, much of the daily putting away of the heavy items will be eliminated, and in many cases, over a period of five years or more, it can become almost fully self-financing in terms of the saving of staff time, which can then be devoted to other important things.

Importantly, where possible, children should have access to continuous outdoor provision. This will almost always be offered in children's centres and larger day nurseries and in schools where there is an EYFS unit made up of nursery and reception classes. This is because in these provision set-ups there will always be at least three staff available, which is the generally accepted minimum staffing requirement for continuous indoor and outdoor provision to be effectively and safely provided. In schools where nursery and reception classes share the outdoor area, and where it is adjacent and easily accessible from both classrooms, then it is possible to share staffing for the outdoor area and so have it continuously available for most of the sessions.

Editor's notes

Whenever you start to think about developing or further developing your outdoor area, you first need to think of the kinds of experiences you want your children to have and how possible and practical these are within the space you have available. Whatever you can do will always depend upon the time and the money you have available. Always remember the old adage when someone says, '*We can't afford to do it,*' the retort is often '*But can we afford not to do it?*'

The EYFS says children should be outdoors as much as they are indoors and that outdoor learning is their entitlement and their need. We do need to do the best we can for our children and sometimes this takes time, possibly several years. But it's no good if we don't have a vision or action plan that we can work towards achieving. Often, when working in this way, we can surprise ourselves that we manage to get the vision into place much earlier than anticipated.

Bibliography and further reading

Bilton, Helen (2002) *Outdoor Play in the Early Years: Management and innovation*. David Fulton Publications.

Design Brief for Developing the Outdoor Environment at the EYFS (2008) Manchester City Council.

Edgington, Margaret (2003) *The Great Outdoors: Developing Children's Learning Through Outdoor Provision*. British Association for Early Childhood Education.

Garrick, Ros (2009) *Playing Outdoors in the Early Years*. Continuum International Publishing Group.

Guidance for the Outdoor Learning Environment in the Foundation Stage (2005) Manchester City Council.

Ouvry, Marjorie (2003) *Exercising Muscles and Minds*. National Children's Bureau.

Warden, Clare (2005) *The Potential of a Puddle*. Mindstretchers.

White, Jan (2007) *Playing and Learning Outdoors. Making Provision for High Quality Experiences in the Outdoor Environment*. Routledge.

It's about more than just trying hard

5

Effective observation, recording and assessment systems

Terry Gould

Observation is the key to finding out what children know and can do. The most effective settings use time in planned and spontaneous ways to observe their children and then use these observations to plan the next steps for children's learning and development.

Having some shared inset sessions on observation and recording helps to ensure each member of the team has a clear shared understanding of the purpose of observation, and from this can develop a shared ethos and consistent approach. So why do we observe children? Before reading this list, try to identify the reasons you do this in your school/setting.

Why we observe children

To help us to understand:

- what they can do and have learned so far
- what they know and understand
- what attitudes and opinions they have
- what likes, dislikes and interests they have
- the ways in which they learn best
- the context in which they learn best
- what they are in the process of learning.

But also to help us to plan and review the curriculum/learning experiences we are offering to children by seeing if . . .

- the provision indoors and outdoors
- the resources and equipment
- the organisation and management (including routines of the day)
- the teaching strategies used

. . . are effectively supporting every child's needs and interests.

It is valuable to discuss as a team how we can observe children. So get that pad out again and make your own list before reading on.

We can observe children by:

- watching what they do
- listening to what they say
- noticing how they behave
- watching their interactions with others
- interacting and talking with them
- raising questions with them
- posing problems for them to consider
- being aware of the context in which children are learning
- recognising their achievements
- collecting and annotating things (or photos of things) they produce/make.

The final thing to consider as an EYFS team is what kinds of observations can we undertake?

Yes, you guessed! Time to get that pad out and write down what you do already in terms of the kinds of observations undertaken in your school/setting, before reading on.

Kinds of observations:

1) informal observations – small notes of incidental things we observe children doing and saying
2) structured observations by targeting
   - individual children
   - a particular workshop area of provision
   - a particular activity
3) time sampling, where notes are made every five minutes
4) observations from videos/DVDs – use made of videos/DVDs taken of children at play and reflected on in detail later.

Next, as a team, it is useful to go through the basic steps of observation.

Basic steps to effective observation and recording

It is imperative that all staff find the time to look, listen and note, and then respond. They need to:

- OBSERVE   be aware, look and listen
- RECORD   what they see and hear
- SHARE   what they have seen and heard
- DECIDE   how to use the recorded information.

Not all observations need to be recorded, only the significant ones. Observations can be recorded on one or more of the following:

- sticky notes
- secretarial-type A5 sized pads
- sticky labels
- formatted observation sheets
- any other viable alternative

and should include:

- WHO – child's name and names of other children, adults
- WHERE – in the room area things occur, e.g. sand, water, book, outdoors, etc.
- WHEN – e.g. time of day: breakfast, morning play, dinnertime, etc.
- WHAT – brief description of what the child does including language used by the child.

Whatever the practitioner writes should be factual and specific:

- objective – not an interpretation
- based on strengths of the child – 'can do' model
- dated and signed where necessary.

One key question I am often asked is: 'How often and how many times a day do practitioners need to complete observations of children?' The simple reply is that there is no definitive answer to the question other than the guideline I always give, in line with good EYFS practice, that: 'Observations should be completed on a daily basis by all practitioners and should never be written simply for the sake of having completed some observations.' Observations should always have the purpose of informing the reader about what children know and can do and leading into planning the next steps in their learning and development.

Since a practitioner cannot write and observe at the same time, notes taken during an observation should be kept to a minimum and observations should be written up as soon as possible after the observation, while the memory of the observation is still fresh and accurate. Practitioners should not try to identify the Development Matters area/s as they write the observation. This can be undertaken later.

▶ Key things to remember when writing observations

- Stick to the facts of what child actually does.
- Be specific and include enough details to 'paint a picture'.
- Make it clear for someone else reading it.
- Make sure it is dated and, if appropriate, signed, and includes the appropriate 'who, what, where and when'.

What practitioners should do:

- Use observations to chart progress/achievements of children – including the compilation of learning journeys.

Use observations to inform planning the next steps for children:

- make observations of all children on an ongoing daily basis
- bring key points from observations to planning meeting/s
- pass completed observations to the child's key person
- key person enters observation into each child's profile and appropriately updates child's individual record of achievement – individual child profiles are updated at least once every 6-8 weeks on a rolling programme (unless this is done with the teacher)
- share observations with parents/carers at regular intervals through child profile reviews which include learning journeys and summary sheets.

Ongoing observations (LOOK, LISTEN and NOTE) – will ensure that practitioners are able to RESPOND appropriately and will:

- get to know their children better
- develop further detailed understanding of a child's development
- be helped to share information with parents
- be able to plan appropriate play and other learning opportunities for children, based on interests and needs
- build on what children know and can already do
- identify any concerns about the child's development.

An observation board, sited on the wall, is a useful means of collating observations. The use of such a board facilitates a range of contributors to the assessment process. Points to consider:

- each child will need to have their own pocket with text/photograph
- observation key messages are displayed
- blank observation formats are accessible close to the board.

Assessment

This can be defined simply as **'The decisions you make using what you observe'** *(EYFS 2007)*.

Assessment is quite simply the decisions you make about children's progress and development based on the things you see and hear. Without observation, no assessment can take place as the two go hand in hand. Reflecting on observations is the start of the assessment process.

The assessment process should consider:

- what a child can do
- what the child needs help with
- what the child is ready to move on to next
- what the child's particular interests are
- how these interests can be used to extend learning.

Assessment decisions should be shared with other involved professionals and parents/carers. By sharing the PLODS (possible lines of direction/next steps) the team, including the child's family, will be better informed and able to support the child moving forwards in a range of contexts. There are no set assessment formats and practitioners are free to develop their own. However, the EYFS Profile is a statutory requirement and has to be completed for all children at the end of their time in the reception class.

> **'Observation and assessment drives the planning process which is the key to making children's learning effective, varied and progressive.'** *(EYFS 2008.)*

The process should always be the same:

OBSERVE ⟶ RECORD ⟶ ASSESS ⟶ PLAN

Editor's notes

The observation, recording and assessment process is the key to understanding how and what children learn, and responding to this by doing something about moving their learning and development forward. It is imperative that all staff in a school, PIV setting or children's centre be supported to become skilled at this. This is one of the first things you may need to consider when aiming to take your practice and provision forwards. This is why I have identified it as one of the five pillars of all EYFS practice and provision.

A challenge occurs where children attend more than one setting. How can the practitioners in such situations work closer together across settings to ensure that what is provided and planned for the child is appropriate and meaningful in each of the settings?

Additionally, are all providers equally valued by all settings or do we sometimes have a culture of thinking that we should take some less seriously than others? For example in some cases the work of some settings (e.g. childminders) and the information records on children is undervalued by other providers at the point of transition.

Bibliography and further reading

Cousins, Jacqui. (2003) *Listening To Four Year Olds: How They Can Help Us Plan Their Care and Education*. National Children's Bureau.

Fisher, Julie. (2007) *Starting from The Child: Teaching and Learning from 3–8*. Open University Press.

Hutchin, Vicky. (2007) *Supporting Every Child's Learning across the Early Years Foundation Stage*. Hodder Education.

Observation, Assessment & Planning in the EYFS: A Toolkit for Manchester's Early Years Practitioners (2009) Manchester City Council.

The Early Years Foundation Stage Guidance (2008) DCFS National Strategies.

The Early Years Toolkit (2001) Salford City Council Salford LA.

Planning it right

6

Using planning to support improved outcomes for all children

Terry Gould

'All planning starts with observing children in order to understand and consider their current interests, development, and learning needs.' *(EYFS 2007)*

'Acknowledging the child as a competent learner should ensure that the starting point for planning an appropriate curriculum is the child's developing skills and understanding.' *(Fisher 2002)*

Observation must form the starting point for all planning. Planning should be based on the principle that children learn most effectively when they are motivated and interested by the activities in which they engage.

To support effective learning through play, practitioners need to:

- plan and resource a challenging learning environment
- support children's learning through planned play activity
- support and extend children's spontaneous play
- support and extend children's language and communication in their play
- support and engage with children's interests.

Planning requires that practitioners not only have a clear understanding of what children need to know and understand and be able to do, but also of how children learn and develop. They must also be flexible with their planning. Planning must reflect the key role practitioners play in taking forward children's learning and development. This should be based on the practitioners'

recognition of the huge impact language has on children's thought and learning, and how this is importantly linked with their sustained shared thinking. EPPE research 2003 (see Bibliography and further reading) has helped to highlight the importance of sustained shared thinking and the centrality of talk in the learning process.

Planning should be:

- clear
- concise
- manageable

and should lead to good progress for all children. It should have due regard to:

- the deployment of staff
- routines and organisation of the day
- the established learning environment.

The planning process should start with the child through **observation** and **assessment** leading into reflection on next steps/PLODS (possible lines of direction) which might include identified opportunities for child-initiated, independent and adult-led learning.

   Effective practice is where practitioners take notice, understand and then **respond** effectively.

Long-term planning

Long-term planning is where we make sure that the statutory requirements, principles and commitments and the *Practice Guidance* of the EYFS are embedded in daily practice. It is the point at which we ensure children's entitlement to a broad and balanced set of learning and development opportunities, through personalised care routines, and a quality learning environment. In this way, it makes important links with the themes and principles of the EYFS.

   At its simplest, this stage of planning outlines an overview of what children will learn and approximately when they will learn it, throughout the year. It ensures appropriate coverage of the curriculum. One of the most effective ways to organise this is to decide which Development Matters, areas or Early Learning Goals will be focused on for specific periods or each half term. The whole team should plan this stage together so as to help to provide checks and balances, so ensuring that the coverage of the required learning and development is appropriately spread.

   Long-term planning should be completed prior to the start of the year and can be repeated each year. Often this is best through a two-year cycle of topics/themes. Once this is completed, it will need reviewing only on an annual basis, at which time any amendments can be made. At the long-term planning stage, where the actual learning will take place does not need to be identified.

Continuous long-term planning for the developed provision areas additionally supports the overview. It identifies learning opportunities, which will continuously be available throughout the year from child-initiated activity. This planning identifies opportunities provided for all children to practise and consolidate existing skills and learn new ones.

Long-term plans are effective only when they reflect the approach and philosophy of the EYFS and embed its principles. All long-term planning is underpinned by the policies of the setting/school.

Long-term planning needs to reflect or include:

- setting/school policies
- EYFS annual development plan
- daily routines and organisation
- continuous planning/provision
- adult roles
- calendar of special events, festivals and celebrations
- and for older children (over-threes) – a broad, thematic plan used flexibly over the year and ideally through a two-year cycle.

Medium-term planning

Medium-term planning bridges the gap between the long-term overview and short-term planning. It provides a projected set of learning outcomes across all six areas of learning through Development Matters, which are used flexibly to meet the on-going needs of all children. It makes the links with the commitments of the EYFS.

It should reflect children's predicted natural interests and is a place where ideas are gathered from staff, children and parents/carers. Learning beyond children's familiar experiences needs to be planned for and carefully based on professional judgement.

In this tier of planning, practitioners will record some of the main details of how, when and where identified learning and development will be delivered. Additionally at this stage the planning needs to identify some ideas for activities that will be used to deliver the learning, and appropriate assessment opportunities for some of these. This does not need to be comprehensive but some activities planned for outdoors can be identified – one way of doing this is simply to highlight these with a green highlighter.

It's important to recognise that any differentiation of activities should not be attempted at this stage as accurate/sufficient information of the required differentiation will not be available at this point in time.

Medium-term planning does not always mean for a fixed period, e.g. Spring Term. Sometimes it can be for a shorter period and should be a flexible period of time during which one or more themes may overlap. It can be used as a broad focus to support learning and development. If themes are used, they should be broad and flexibly used across the year and chosen in relation to children's interests, known or predicted, and planned from the starting point of what children already know. These plans are effective only when they are used not too rigidly. Additional learning outcomes may be identified and some projected outcomes may not be taught as planned. Using medium-term plans in this way helps to make them a responsive working document.

Medium-term planning needs to include or reflect:

- priority next steps for learning based on previously identified learning outcomes
- links to all six areas of learning and development
- learning outcomes linked to (i) Development Matters and (ii) Look, Listen and Note
- details of partnership working with parents/carers and involved agencies
- on-going whole team reflection on practice in line with the themes and commitments of the EYFS
- identified special events and celebrations – visits and visitors
- for children aged three and above, the possible use of broad, flexibly-used themes as a starting point for planning.

There is a growing trend within some local authorities to eliminate the medium-term planning tier by combining the long and medium-term plans. This has the purpose of shifting the emphasis of planning onto the short-term tier, which has the most impact on outcomes for children's learning and development.

Short-term planning

Short-term planning is a direct response to observations and assessments and is directly informed by medium-term planning. It indicates the weekly organisation and coverage of development matters or Early Learning Goals through the following:

- routine of the day
- child-initiated activities
- focused activities
- group/circle times
- targeted activities
- enhancements planned for the developed learning areas
- deployment of practitioners and any unqualified helpers
- evaluation of learning
- assessment opportunities.

The Fabulous Foundation Stage

Short-term planning should be sufficiently detailed and include appropriate differentiation. It provides a focused set of stage-appropriate learning outcomes, quality experiences and activities, and a balance of opportunities for each child to engage in child-initiated, independent and adult-led activities across each day.

Short-term is the most important tier of planning because it relates to the next steps for individual children based on their identified learning and development needs through observational-based assessment. It should be a very responsive working document which involves setting out what is to be implemented in everyday practice on a daily or weekly basis within the broad EYFS framework so as to meet the individual needs, stages of development and interests of children. To be successful it needs to be a working document and therefore should be amended or changed as necessary to meet the needs of children and to accommodate spontaneous learning opportunities, e.g. when it snows.

The short-term planning should cover activities for both indoors and outdoors and should identify where the activities should take place. As with the medium-term planning, activities taking place outdoors should be identified. An effective way of achieving this is simply to highlight those activities using a green highlighter.

Short-term planning needs to be flexible enough to value and cater for spontaneous, child-initiated activities. Where it is seen that the child-initiated activity is of more value than that planned by the adult, planning should simply be altered/amended and the originally planned activity cancelled or postponed.

This tier of planning is at its most effective when it includes contributions from the whole staff team which reflect observational-based assessments of children and the views and contributions of parents/carers and children. Medium-term planning can evolve and change as a consequence of short-term planning. The process of short-term planning makes links with the observation and assessment cycle.

Short-term planning should include:

- identified learning outcomes
- environmental enhancements as required, with links to learning opportunities within the daily routines to support individual children where appropriate, e.g. gradual admission
- daily group times to include story times, three or five a day story/poem programme and for children over three years phonics/Letters and Sounds type activities
- daily focused activities
- targeted learning outcomes for individual children, groups of children or across areas of learning
- differentiation including that for children identified with SEN
- staff deployment with opportunities to record observations of child-initiated play or independent learning.

Since time is needed for quality observations of children, short-term planning, although needing to be detailed, should not and need not be over-burdensome or time-consuming for practitioners. The following short-term planning formats are tried and tested and can be freely used or adapted.

Learning outcomes	Activities	Teaching	Resources/ language	Assessment
How does this build on previous learning? What do you expect the children to learn? What are the targets for this group? (refer to Developmental Matters)	What will the children be doing? How will they engage with the learning?	Outline the teaching approach, differentiation and groupings.	Key resources to be used. Key language to be modelled and promoted.	Indicate any informal assessments to be undertaken and any formal assessments related to the planning. Use Look, Listen and Note section of the EYFS
Evaluation and additional observational notes				
Group/circle time Short-term planning				

EYFS short-term planning

Nursery/Reception (circle) Focused activity (Non-assessed)

Practitioner _____ Date _____

Learning objective	Differentiation	Look, Listen and Note
	1. 2. 3.	

Description of activity

Resources	Key vocabulary

Observational notes

EYFS Short-term planning

Nursery/Reception (circle) Focused activity (Assessed)

Practitioner _____ Date _____

Learning objective	Differentiation	Look, Listen and Note
	1. 2. 3.	

Description of activity

Resources	Key vocabulary

Name	Outcome	Next steps

CATCH UP and STRETCH Short-term targeted planning			
Group _____ W/C _____			
Learning objective	**Activity and where it takes place**	**Children**	**Evaluation/Notes**
What do you want the children to be able to do?	What will it look like?	Initials of children to be targeted.	What was the outcome? What were the children able to do?

NB Activities planned for the outdoor area are to be highlighted in green.

Explanatory notes for Catch up and Stretch (CUS) targeted planning

The above CUS should be based on weekly staff discussion/meetings and observational summaries of children's identified needs, and targeted at specific children; although all children are welcome to join in with these as well as those targeted.

The activities planned will take place in a developed area, either indoors or outdoors, whichever is seen as the optimum location for the child. The identifying of targeted children and the planning of these activities is a whole team effort and will be supported by the key person role.

The activities will be managed and supported by the practitioner acting in the targeter/manager role over the week.

From experience, many of these activities will tend to be targeted at the lower achievers who need extra input from the adults although there will be times when other children are also targeted from the MA and HA groupings.

The targeted children will often be encouraged to engage with the activity on more than one occasion over the week.

Over time, using this way of working, will be opportunities to narrow the gap between the lowest 20 per cent achievers and the median of the group in attainment.

The following pages represent one format of addressing long and medium-term planning jointly. This would be accompanied by any topic webs etc., as identified earlier in this chapter.

Settings will highlight the ELGs to be worked towards for each specific period, such as half a term, using different colours which could relate to the season e.g. Autumn 1: orange, Autumn 2: brown etc etc. There will be some that will be on-going, e.g. in the area of Dispositions and Attitudes – excited and motivated to learn – and these will be left in white indicating that these are ongoing aims.

Creative Development	
EXPLORING MEDIA AND MATERIALS	
C1	Explores colour, texture, shape, form and space in two or three dimensions
MUSIC	
C2	Recognises and explores how sounds can be changed, sing simple songs from memory, recognise repeated sounds and sound patterns and match movements to music
IMAGINATION	
C3	Use their imagination in art and design, music, dance, imaginative and role play and stories
RESPONDING TO EXPERIENCES AND EXPRESSING AND COMMUNICATING IDEAS	
C4	Respond in a variety of ways to what they see, hear, smell, feel and touch
C5	Express and communicate their ideas, thoughts and feelings by using a widening range of materials, suitable tools, imaginative and role play, movement, designing and making and a variety of songs and musical instruments
Communication Language and Literacy	
LANGUAGE AND COMMUNICATION	
CLL1	Interacts with others, negotiating plans and activities and taking turns in conversation
CLL2	Enjoy listening to and using spoken language and readily turns to it in their play and learning
CLL3	Sustains attentive listening, responding to what they have heard by regular comments questions or actions
CLL4	Listens with enjoyment and responds to stories songs and other music, rhymes and poems and make up their own stories, rhymes, songs and poems
CLL5	Extend their vocabulary, exploring the meanings and sounds of new words
CLL6	Speaks clearly and audibly with confidence and control and shows awareness of the listener e.g by their use of conventions such as greetings, please and thank you

THINKING	
CLL7	Uses language to imagine and recreate roles and experiences
CLL8	Uses talk to organise, sequence and clarify thinking, ideas, feelings and events

LINKING SOUNDS AND LETTERS	
CLL9	Hear and say sounds in words in the order in which they occur
CLL10	Link sounds to letters, naming and sounding the letters of the alphabet
CCL11	Use their phonic knowledge to write simple regular words and make phonetically plausible attempts at more complex words

READING	
CLL12	Explore and experiment with sounds, words and texts
CLL13	Retell narratives in the correct sequence drawing on the language patterns of stories
CLL14	Read a range of familiar and common words and simple sentences independently
CLL15	Knows that print carries meaning and in English is read from left to right and top to bottom
CLL16	Shows an awareness of the elements of stories such as a main character, sequence of events, and openings and how information can be found in fiction texts to answer questions about where, who, why and how

WRITING AND HANDWRITING	
CLL17	Use their phonic knowledge to write simple regular words and make phonetically plausible attempts at more complex words
CLL18	Attempts writing for a variety of purposes, using features of different forms such as lists, stories, and instructions
CLL19	Write their own names and other things such as labels and captions and begin to form simple sentences sometimes using punctuation

Physical Development

MOVEMENT	
P1	Move with confidence, imagination and in safety
P2	Move with control and coordination
P3	Travel around, under, over and through balancing and climbing equipment

SENSE OF SPACE	
P4	Show awareness of space, of themselves and of others

HEALTH AND BODILY AWARENESS	
P5	Recognises the importance of keeping healthy and those things which contribute to this
P6	Recognises the changes that happen to their bodies when they are active

The Fabulous Foundation Stage

	USING EQUIPMENT
P7	Uses a range of small and large equipment

	USING TOOLS AND MATERIALS
P8	Handles tools, objects, construction and malleable safely and with increasing control

Problem Solving, Reasoning and Numeracy

	NUMBERS AS LABELS AND FOR COUNTING
M1	Say and use number names in familiar contexts
M2	Count reliably up to ten everyday objects
M3	Recognise numbers 1–9
M4	Use developing mathematical ideas to solve practical problems

	CALCULATING
M5	In practical activities and discussions begin to use the vocabulary involved in adding and subtracting
M6	Use language such as more or less to compare two numbers
M7	Find one more or one less than a number 1–10
M8	Begin to relate addition to combining groups of objects and subtraction to taking away

	SHAPE SPACE AND MEASURES
M9	Use language such as greater, smaller, heavier or lighter to compare quantities
M10	Talk about, recognise and create simple patterns
M11	Use language such as circle or bigger to describe the shape and size of solids and flat shapes
M12	Use everyday words to describe position
M13	Use developing mathematical ideas to solve practical problems

Knowledge and Understanding of the World

	EXPLORATION AND INVESTIGATION
KU1	Investigate objects and materials by using all their senses as appropriate
KU2	Find out about and identify some features of living things, objects and events they observe
KU3	Look closely at similarities and differences, patterns and change
KU4	Asks questions about why things happen and how things work

	DESIGNING AND MAKING
KU5	Builds and constructs with a wide range of objects selecting appropriate resources and adapting their work where necessary
KU6	Select the tools and techniques they need to shape, assemble and join the materials together

	INFORMATION AND COMMUNICATION TECHNOLOGY
KU7	Find out about and identify the uses of everyday technology and communication technology and programmable toys to support their learning

	SENSE OF TIME AND PLACE
KU8	Find out about past and present events in their own lives and in those of their families and other people they know
KU9	Observe, find out about and identify features in the place they live and the natural world
KU10	Find out about their environment and talk about those features they like and dislike

	CULTURES AND BELIEFS
KU11	Begin to know about their own cultures and beliefs and those of other people

Personal, Social and Emotional Development

	DISPOSITIONS AND ATTITUDES
PSE1	Continue to be interested, excited and motivated to learn
PSE2	Be confident to try new activities, initiate ideas and speak in a familiar group
PSE3	Maintain attention, concentration, and sit quietly when appropriate

	SELF-CONFIDENCE AND SELF-ESTEEM
PSE4	Responds to significant experiences, showing a range of feelings when appropriate
PSE5	Have a developing awareness of their own needs, views and feelings and be sensitive to the feelings of others
PSE6	Have a developing respect of their own cultures and beliefs and those of other people

	MAKING RELATIONSHIPS
PSE7	Form good relationships with adults and peers
PSE8	Works as part of a group, taking turns and sharing fairly and understanding that there need to be agreed values and codes of behaviour for groups of people including adults and children to work harmoniously

BEHAVIOUR AND SELF-CONTROL	
PSE9	Understands what is right and wrong and why
PSE10	Consider the consequences of their words and actions for themselves and others
SELF-CARE	
PSE11	Dress and undress independently and manage their own hygiene
PSE12	Select own activities and resources independently
SENSE OF COMMUNITY	
PSE13	Understands that people have different needs, views, cultures and beliefs which need to be treated with respect
PSE14	Understand that they can expect others to treat their needs, views, beliefs and cultures with respect

Autumn 1	
Autumn 2	
Spring 1	
Spring 2	
Summer 1	
Summer 2	

Definition of some common terms

- Continuous provision: provision in which children have independent access throughout the year, so that they can repeat and consolidate and build on experiences at their own pace.
- Enhanced provision: provision which has been enhanced with specific resources aimed at encouraging learning to take a particular direction.
- Focused provision: direct teaching with planned learning intentions, which are appropriately differentiated for small numbers of children.
- Group/circle time: direct teaching with planned learning intentions, which are appropriately differentiated, for larger numbers of children.
- Differentiation: meeting the needs of all children by ensuring that their different learning needs and stages of development are catered for appropriately and effectively.

Editor's notes

If we are not careful, we can quite easily make our planning over-burdensome and then not have the time and capacity to follow the interests and needs of our children as required by the EYFS. Where possible, practitioners are advised to slim down on planning formats and keep systems simple, so as to free up time and energy to do what is the most important – support children's learning and development, starting with observations of what they know and can do.

The key message of this chapter is precisely that 'less is often more!' We do need to constantly remind ourselves (and colleagues) that we do not have to write down everything that we plan for our children, and that it is not desirable to do so, in terms of the effective use of our time. Most of our planning should be a response to our children's interests and what they need to learn and should directly impact on outcomes for them. When we drill down, there are only two generic things we need to do within the EYFS, and these are:

1. Deliver teaching and learning through good practice
2. Improve and maintain outcomes for children.

(This is not to say that these two things are not complex or that in some cases they are always easy to achieve.)

Our planning should directly support both of the above and enable us to successfully implement the themes, principles and commitments of the EYFS, if it is to be meaningful and effective.

Bibliography and further reading

Fisher, Julie. (2002) *Starting from The Child: Teaching and Learning from 3–8*. Open University Press.

Hutchin, Vicky. (2007) *Supporting Every Child's Learning Across The Early Years Foundation Stage*. Hodder Education.

Observation, Assessment & Planning in the EYFS: A Toolkit for Manchester's Early Years Practitioners. (2009) Manchester City Council.

The Early Years Foundation Stage Guidance (2008) DCFS National Strategies.

The Early Years Toolkit (2001) Salford City Council Salford LA.

Let's hear it for the boys! 7

A focus on supporting and encouraging boys' early writing

Terry Gould

Planning should be based on the principle that children learn most effectively when they are motivated and interested by the activities in which they engage. Ongoing regular observations of children's interests, needs and learning styles should be used to plan activities that stimulate, challenge and inspire and nowhere is this more significant than in supporting boys as early writers.

The main aspects which practitioners need to address with the early writer are:

- Fine motor development
- Attitude to writing
- Composition of writing
- The purpose of writing
- Phonic knowledge.

To be able to develop skills effectively with children, the team needs to understand the stages of development in writing and know exactly where each child is in terms of their development as a writer, through observational-based assessment. This I term 'tuning into children'.

What do the boys need?

Boys need practitioners who understand them, through tuning into their interests and needs. For many, some of the next questions will perhaps be:

What is meant by tuning in?
How should we do this?

How we tune into children as writers is about providing them with modelled, shared and guided writing in ways which are meaningful to them and are linked to their own interests.

Modelled writing

Boys need to see the writing process valued and used by adults and other children around them in meaningful ways and for a real purpose – male role models are especially useful. In modelled writing the practitioner is in control of the process. He/she demonstrates how ideas become written words by thinking aloud so that children can see into the mind of a skilled writer. (The thought process, decisions and writing belong to the practitioner.) Modelled writing should happen daily through:

- – being cross-curricular
- – taking place in all areas of the indoor and outdoor learning environment
- – being short, simple and sometimes one word
- – providing interest to boys.

Static models

A quality literate environment has models of writing at child height, e.g. labels, captions, letters etc., and should ensure it sufficiently engages boys.

Shared writing

In shared writing, children participate in a planned activity to produce a joint piece of writing. The role of the adult is to encourage and motivate children within an unthreatening context. This needs to ensure a focus on things that boys are interested in and that the ideas come from the boys' observed interests where possible e.g. let's make a pirate map.

Guided writing

In guided writing children practise their writing with guidance and support. It is an opportunity to put into practice what they have been learning in modelled and shared writing sessions. (The thought process, decisions and writing belong to the child, guided by the practitioner. Again this needs to be 'boy friendly' and relate to boys' interests.)

Independent writing opportunities

In independent writing children practise and consolidate their writing skills at every opportunity within the Foundation Stage environment. They develop strong self-images as purposeful and effective writers. This is probably one of the main areas where we can attract boys to the process if we get it right.

The writing may not be with traditional pencil and paper, but through innovative approaches such as writing with sticks in mud outdoors or writing secret messages which disappear, or in a black flat builder's tray with shaving foam and fingers or with washing-up liquid bottles squirting out water to write, or water pots and brushes on flagstones.

Practitioners need to engage with boys to assist all four types of support for writing:

- modelled
- shared
- guided
- independent.

They can do this most effectively by ensuring that the learning environment, provided and maintained (indoors and outdoors), constitutes a responsive curriculum to boys' individual and group interests and needs.

Ensuring a responsive curriculum that meets all children's writing development needs

Young children, including boys, learn best when the teaching closely addresses their interests and stage of development and this is what is meant by providing a responsive curriculum – one which responds to them as writers. Hence, it requires practitioners to provide rich and stimulating play environments, e.g. role-play area, writing area, construction area, outdoor writing den, etc. in which boys have the opportunity to engage in writing which is meaningful for them. It also requires practitioners to be mindful of the fact that children need:

- adults to provide relevant and interesting activities which prompt children to participate in and explore new ideas
- to have sufficient time to explore print and to consolidate writing skills
- to have sufficient space and appropriate resources to write for their own purpose.

Boys will engage much more with things in which they are interested.

In order to provide this responsive curriculum, adults will need to know about boys' writing behaviours and what these mean. They will have to have observed boys' writing behaviours including where and how often they write and then work as a team to:

- Ensure they all understand the function of children writing.
- Discuss the implications for practice including the support the boys need.
- Provide exciting and meaningful opportunities for boys to write.
- Enable boys to see themselves as writers.

Practitioners need to have an understanding that underpins the writing opportunities provided which includes the recognition that it is important that boys are:

- not totally dependent on 'copy' writing
- encouraged to see themselves as writers, not dependent on adults
- not asked to overwrite as this does little to support them as real writers and can in fact have an adverse effect on their progress.

A copied piece of writing tells us little about the child's ability as a writer, except how well they can copy. Also, too frequent copying most often causes children to think less about the way words are constructed and the patterns of letters in words. This is the reason why children who only or mainly 'copy' write often develop an accuracy hang-up, including becoming frightened of putting pencil to paper without the practitioner doing it first.

Practitioners who support children with their independent writing enable children to see themselves as real writers and develop a positive attitude towards writing. If practitioners agree that writing is an important life skill, then their role should ensure that the most effective ways of supporting boys in this are employed.

There are many effective ways to achieve this but the use of the following can prove highly effective:

- Create 'writing to go' boxes with a gender slant towards boys, e.g. pirate ship writing box.
- Create an improved literate environment with role-play areas being more boy friendly e.g. builder's yard.
- Provide clipboards in all areas.
- Provide writing belts.

To be good writers, boys first need to be good thinkers and good talkers. Early on in their development as writers, boys, like girls, will benefit from the adult acting as scribe whether this is at home or in the setting. Scribing for children has effectively and successfully taken place for many years. Children often have far more to say than they are given credit for and where the need to undertake the difficult transcription process is removed, their thinking and speaking skills demonstrate their creative abilities as storywriters.

A project undertaken in Manchester in 2006 used the ICT software 'Tizzy's First Tools' to support children as storywriters. The key findings were that:

- It connected with boys and girls as writers – they wrote about what interested them.
- It enabled them to write real stories allowing them to unlock their ideas and see themselves as real authors.
- Boys and girls were encouraged to use the writing process of think it – say it – write it – read it.
- They were enabled to see the connections between their thoughts, the words they spoke, and the written word.

- Children, including a large number of boys who had previously lacked interest in more traditional writing activities, were motivated to engage in the project.
- Boys often drew very detailed pictures relating to their stories – often much more than girls.
- Boys and girls often wrote about things they had heard or read through good quality storybooks.

Knowing whether or not things are going well with writing in your setting may appear easy to judge. However, in some settings use of some type of self-evaluation process can be an important factor in accurately finding this out. The following questions may be of use in this process.

Do the boys in your setting…

- write spontaneously for their own purposes?
- enjoy writing on their own and with others?
- talk readily and enthusiastically about their own or other people's writing?
- ask questions about what writing says?
- want to participate in writing activities?
- write at home?
- talk with their parents about writing?

When we begin to ensure that we meet the needs and interests of boys and girls then our provision for writing will be truly inclusive. It is only when this happens that we can feel certain that the potential of all children, including the boys, can be fully realised.

Editor's notes

Engaging boys as writers is about tuning in to their interests and needs. We need to be mindful that the brains of boys and girls are wired differently. This has implications for the differing ways in which they may approach the writing process. Boys are often interested in being loud and noisy and as such, may often prefer characters who appear to display similar characteristics, such as pirates or soldiers. We need to engage with boys in more meaningful ways than we may do at present, so that they can see how the four modes of speaking, listening, reading and writing all fit in together as communication tools. Using technology can impact significantly on the success of this.

We must remember that engaging in writing is something that grows with us throughout childhood and beyond. If we are to encourage boys to write we need to ensure that we provide them with a wide range of writing opportunities that make writing meaningful and purposeful. A useful exercise would be to walk around your setting and identify how many writing opportunities there are on a daily basis that you know would attract the boys. If there are not many then the way forward is clear – make sure that there are! Writing can be seen as a bit like riding a bike; the more you do it, the better you get at it. Our boys need to engage in writing to get better at it!

Bibliography and further reading

Browne, A. (2009) *Developing Language and Literacy 3–8 (3rd edition)* Sage Publications Ltd.

EYFS Guidance (2007) DCFS National Strategies.

Gould, Terry (English 4–11, pp17–20 Spring 2006) 'Using ICT as a tool to support children at the foundation stage in developing their skills as authors'.

Rich, D. (2002) *More than words – Children Developing Communication Language and Literacy.* British Association For Early Education.

Key Elements of Effective Practice (2005) DCFS National Strategies

Whitehead, Marian. (1999) *Supporting Language and Literacy Development in the Early Years.* Open University Press.

Writing Matters (2006) Manchester Education Partnership. Manchester City Council.

Press it, turn it, switch it, move it

ICT as a tool to support learning and development

Terry Gould

The EYFS contains 69 Early Learning Goals of which just one relates directly to ICT. This is contained within the section of Knowledge and Understanding of the World and states that children should:

'find out about and identify the uses of everyday technology and use information technology and programmable toys to support their learning.'

This goal can be split into three distinct strands:

- use ICT equipment to support their learning
- use simple switch, remote control and programmable toys
- develop an awareness and use of everyday technology in the real world.

To ensure that children receive their entitlement to good quality ICT experiences in each of these strands, children need:

- sufficient access to age-appropriate resources
- well-informed adults who support children's learning effectively from an early age.

To support the achievement of the above, practitioners should ensure that there are ICT based learning opportunities in:

A **The continuous provision** i.e. computer/s and appropriate software based around the children's daily learning environment, as well as a range of other ICT devices in various areas of provision, such as a cassette player/ recorder in the listening area, or an electronic till in the role-play shop, or a telephone in the home corner, etc.

B **The enhanced provision** e.g. a scanner and calculator added to the shop, walkie-talkies added to the fire-fighter outdoor resource box, a metal detector added to the airport role-play area, etc.

C **The focused provision** e.g. the adult shows children how to use walkie-talkies or new computer software, or the adult works with a group on tasks involving a BEEBOT robot.

It is important to offer as wide a range of opportunities and resources as possible so that young children can start finding out and making connections. All ICT devices are basically response toys of differing complexities. Children's natural interest in pressing buttons, turning knobs and clicking switches complements their interest in sounds and music. Many will be fascinated by musical keyboards and DVD/tape players and recorders, along with pretend domestic appliances, from vacuum cleaners that 'whoosh', microwaves that 'ping' and washing machines that 'whirr' and other tools that mimic the real thing and have moving parts and make sounds, such as drills and saws.

Many toys are battery operated and children can be helped to understand that when the battery goes flat the toy needs a new or re-charged battery. Remote-control cars and other types of vehicle use batteries and these are always of great interest to the young child. However, it is important that children should be offered these in a differentiated way, so as to support early understanding e.g. for the younger child – items with a single forwards and backwards control, and then, once they have mastered this, they can move onto resources with more advanced remote control functions of left and right.

Observations of children using ICT toys and devices including computers will be the main way of finding out what they know and can do in relation to this aspect of learning. Developing learning journeys with digital images can be used to record how children are learning and developing. ICT toys and devices provide a rich learning tool because of the intrinsic interest they provide for the young child and the 'magical qualities' they present both indoors and outdoors.

ICT does not just support knowledge and understanding of the world but enhances learning and development in all six areas of learning:

- Communication, Language and Literacy e.g. ICT is effective in supporting the development of language and literacy.
- Problem Solving, Reasoning and Numeracy e.g. ICT based activities can help to reinforce and develop the concept of number and calculating skills.
- Personal, Social and Emotional Development e.g. using ICT devices puts the child in control, offering a sense of autonomy. A trial and error approach involving exploration and investigation is often adopted which promotes problem solving within scenarios where it feels safe to make mistakes.
- Physical development e.g. many toys and devices support fine motor skills

- Creative development e.g. ICT is often a catalyst for creativity in a range of activities such as music and dance.
- Knowledge and understanding of the world e.g. ICT can support the process of exploration and investigation with open-ended experiences where the process is as important as the product.

The breadth and variety of learning opportunities in all workshop-type areas can be improved through the addition of ICT resources and devices. These include:

1) **Listening area:**
   - listening player/recorder
   - headphones
   - electronic musical instruments and sound toys
   - talking books
   - computer
   - mini voice recorders.

2) **Sensory area:**
   - switch operated light sources
   - bubble tubes
   - musical touch pads
   - musical mobiles.

3) **Book area:**
   - talking photo albums
   - electronic books
   - torches for book dens.

4) **Small world area:**
   - Bee Bot mini robots
   - calming creatures, e.g. pretend puppies
   - digital camera
   - Builder Bots
   - mini remote cars and trucks.

5) **Songs and rhymes/performing arts area:**
   - karaoke machine
   - floor keyboard stepper
   - microphones
   - CD player
   - tape recorder
   - mini electronic organ
   - digital drum set
   - recordable postcards

- digital books
- electric typewriters
- telephone
- torches.

6) **Role-play area:**
   - electronic till
   - electronic scales
   - play television
   - iron
   - vacuum cleaner
   - microwave oven
   - computer
   - telephone
   - fax
   - photocopier
   - music player.

7) **Problem solving, reasoning and numeracy area:**
   - electronic floor mats
   - maths mat challenge
   - talking photo albums made into number books
   - bubble buggies
   - light boxes
   - Bee Bot mini robots and floor mats.

8) **Water area:**
   - mini hovercraft
   - mini submarine
   - remote control boat
   - underwater camera.

9) **Investigative area:**
   - computer
   - digital microscopes
   - digital camera
   - torches wind up and battery operated
   - digital magnifying glasses
   - sound and light toys and devices.

10) **Construction area:**
   - digital camera to record models made
   - builders mini site tools
   - Builder Bots
   - tinkering box of old ICT objects to take apart and put back together.

The Fabulous Foundation Stage

11) **ICT area:**
- computers, printers and speakers
- remote-control toys and devices
- touch screens
- I bugs.

12) **Sand area:**
- mini hand held metal detectors
- larger metal detectors
- digital camera.

13) **Malleable area:**
- microwave oven
- mini digital timers.

14) **Creative area:**
- light box
- digital camera.

15) **Outdoor Area:**
- outdoor webcams
- speed cameras – made with and by children
- dance mats
- wireless outdoor cameras
- walkie talkies
- musical mats
- mini traffic lights
- petrol pumps
- torches
- digicams/Tuffcams
- large remote control vehicles
- bird box cameras
- digital cameras
- hand held extending metal detectors
- cassette player/recorders
- mini weather stations
- karaoke machine
- play electronic tools e.g. hammer drill for road works
- mini hovercrafts
- voice changer megaphones
- electronic mini pressure washers
- microphone voice recorder.

All of these can be obtained through specialist suppliers such as the TTS Group based in Nottingham, or others.

Editor's notes

ICT is much more than simply being about computers, and the importance of ICT in the lives of young children cannot be overstated. The future for all children will involve ICT but at a level perhaps none of us can yet comprehend. Hence, ICT skills are likely to lead to workplace skills of the future but for the present (the today in the child's life) they are skills that help them to engage in playful fun. ICT opens doors and creates possibilities for the active young child on the move. Additionally, ICT can be very supportive of a wide range of communication skills. ICT can support almost all the other Early Learning Goals in exciting ways, including writing, problem solving, reasoning, numeracy and creativity, as we have seen in the previous chapter.

Bibliography and further reading

O'Hara, Mark. (2004) *ICT in the Early Years*. Continuum International Publishing Ltd.

Guidance for the use of ICT in the EYFS Manchester Education Partnership (2007) Manchester City Council.

Siraj-Blatchford, Iram and Siraj-Blatchford, John (2003) 'More than just computers' *Early Education*.

Gould, Terry. (Spring 2006) 'Using ICT as a tool to support children at the foundation stage in developing their skills as authors'. English 4–11 pp17–20.

I know who she takes after 9

Reflections on PSE in the EYFS through personal experiences, and the part it plays in life-long learning, health and well-being

Denise Ellis

A personal introduction

Much has been written about the influence of the socio-economic make-up of our home background on educational achievement; perhaps less on how the attitudes and dispositions of parents, primary carers and educational practitioners affect our personal, social and emotional development as we move towards adulthood, and how these in turn play the major part, as we plot children's progress throughout their education into adulthood.

We can often feel helpless when we consider what impact we might have on the socio-economic status of children's homes, but do we give enough consideration to how we can encourage the aspirations and self-esteem of our children and their families by our support, encouragement and motivation?

To explore the impact of this, I looked back at my own childhood and the influence of my parents, and reflected how their attitudes and dispositions helped to mould the person I became, as I grew up from my earliest years under the age of five, and beyond.

My father was by trade a carpenter and joiner. He loved his job and as I grew up he would constantly say: 'When I go, my legacy will be my helping to make houses for people to live in'. He valued fully what he did, and never failed to encourage my own pursuits.

For me, his legacy was much more. He was, as my own daughter now says, in today's terms, a good example of active citizenship. He wrote poetry, putting down on paper his concerns about the planet, the ills inflicted on the third world and the importance of caring about politics locally, nationally and globally. Too old to be recruited for the Second World War, he volunteered, and would talk fondly about friendships made. After the war, he worked tirelessly for voluntary groups which included Freedom from Hunger, War on Want and the Campaign for Nuclear Disarmament, and was an honorary member of the United Nations Association. He was a school governor, and for me, never missed a parents' evening! Most of all, I knew that he cared both for me and about my educational opportunities, then and for the future.

His father before him had been a town councillor, school inspector, reader of Shakespeare and hobby poet. He undoubtedly inspired my own father by his interests and attitudes to life.

My mother had come from quite humble beginnings. Her father had been killed on the Somme, leaving her still a baby. Growing up in London, in shared rooms with a lone parent had been tough, with food in short supply, and very little stimulus at home.

Her motivation, once she left London, had been that only through hard work would she achieve a better lifestyle for herself and those around her, and this she eventually achieved. Like my father, she took on a practical job which for her was making fireworks.

So here was I, brought up in a home where I was expected to be a Good Citizen and Hard Worker if I was to make progress in life. These were the attitudes and dispositions, be they right or wrong, that existed for me and influenced how I was dealt with as I grew up.

However well I have taken this on is for others to decide, but I am convinced that I have and will never escape the influence that my parents had on my own personal, social and emotional development, from being a young child, as expectations and barriers towards my own behaviour were set. The key elements of their support, however, were the encouragement, support and interest they always showed which for many of our children may well be lacking.

I am not sure which socio-economic scale my parents slotted into but I know in terms of my own personal, social and emotional development I had a good start in life. I was lucky.

Others may recognise the many negative factors of their upbringing and this in itself is for many individuals a motivation for their future life. Undoubtedly, this is not the easiest route towards quality personal, social and emotional development and not one we would ideally wish to choose for our children. For all children, we hope that life starts in a loving family where cuddles, comfort and play help to lay the foundations.

Within our role as educational practitioners we should never lose sight of those children who come from some of our more challenging and disaffected families. For these, our job is more difficult. We need to involve multi-agency teams and that wider world of professionals as identified in the EYFS, as we endeavour to achieve the best outcomes for all of the children in our care.

Supporting the process

For those children coming into our schools and settings, we cannot ignore the influences that they have experienced at home. The environment and opportunities that we offer are open to all of our children equally but as we support children's personal, social and emotional development we cannot ignore how children's behaviour will be affected by a variety of influences.

How can we best support this from an early stage and throughout the educational process towards adulthood? What examples must we set as individual practitioners, within our teams and through the ethos that we create within our settings and schools? Research has shown that the way in which children control their emotions and get along with others is a more significant factor in children's success than their individual IQ. Quality personal, social and emotional development is fundamental if we are to  develop attitudes in our young children which will serve them throughout their life-long learning.

As Early Years practitioners, we hope that the relationships that we develop with families will encourage them to foster similar links as the child moves through the primary and secondary stages of education, and will motivate parents and carers to value education and the quality outcomes which it can promote for their child.

The National Strategy's guidance documents SEAL (Social Emotional Aspects of Learning 2006) and SEAD (Social Emotional Aspects of Development 2008) support this aspect.

Let us consider three parts of the process:

- **the ethos we provide**
- **the communications we establish**
- **the support for learning we encourage.**

I often consider these elements as a traffic light system.

Red: the ethos

The ethos within the environment we create is the RED LIGHT that stops our children, their parents and carers as they begin their learning journey with us and develops their first impressions of what the future could hold.

For us to identify the positive ethos of any environment we need look no further as adults than the last unfamiliar pub, restaurant, shop or social gathering that we entered. How did we feel entering as strangers and how did the ethos of the place contribute to our feelings?

Was it an experience we look back on with pleasure?

Was it the smile that greeted us or the few welcoming words by others which boosted our confidence?

How would we feel about going there again?

As practitioners working within our schools and settings ...

- Are we happy to be there and enjoy the job that we do?
- Do we act as a positive role model?
- Do we give positive encouragement to all children in our care?
- Do we provide positive images through the displays, books and resources we offer, which will support and promote children's emotional moral, spiritual and social development alongside their intellectual development?
- Do we, in fact, create the appropriate climate within that room?

Action points

Model positive attitudes between colleagues by the responses that you give to each other:

- Give every child in your care a daily smile!
- Show the child how much you value their contributions and help.

To foster these elements we need to consider the following:

- The attitudes of those within our team, our joint vision and our clear goals of how we all want our school or setting to be.
- Our respect for individual contributions, valuing the strengths and talents of our children, staff, parents /carers, the multi-agency professionals or members of the child's wider world with whom we work.
- How willing are we to be open-minded, to expand our knowledge, and listen to the beliefs and viewpoints of others?
- How strongly to respond if a viewpoint expressed is inappropriate and unacceptable?

The Fabulous Foundation Stage

- How well have we established an environment which physically makes all our children and adults feel safe and secure?

Do we ever get that second chance to make a first impression?

Amber: communications

Throughout the time that the child is with us the AMBER LIGHT identifies the ongoing communications that we make with our families.

Our first communication with parents/carers and the children in our care will in many cases be verbal and determine how they are made to feel on arrival. Do we in fact display the qualities of good speaking and listening skills that we know we should foster with families and which in turn make our children feel secure?

As practitioners working within our schools and settings:

- Do we show real interest and interaction with genuine warmth?
- Does our attitude and disposition encourage our parents/carers and children to want to communicate?
- Do we recognise the needs of others as they enter this new environment which may hold for some the challenges of past anxieties?
- Do we communicate in a non-opinionated and jargon-free way so as to be unthreatening to others?
- Do we provide social and non-threatening events which enable parents, carers and children to get to know each other in a relaxed climate?
- Do we allow our children opportunities to negotiate with others, expressing their own individual feelings and emotions?

Action points

- Give some positive response to the parent/carer question 'How has he/she been to-day?'
- Phone or email the hard-to-reach or working parent.
- Consider activities which will encourage links with dads and male family members.

For our young children, the key person role strongly promoted within the early years should be that person through whom quality communication can support children's personal and emotional well being – a practitioner who is focused on the child's needs and cares about them and their family.

Much has been written about the value of quality attachment and although the role of the practitioner may change as a child grows, the value of attachment and quality relationships is life-long. Good relationships within families, friends, colleagues and others through which we can communicate often determines how well we cope and adjust to many of the issues life has to throw at us, as we move from childhood to adulthood. There is much truth in the adage 'A problem shared is a problem halved'.

As we get to know our children and their families, a regular free-flow of written communications can reassure them of how settled and happy their children are. Parents and carers who feel in touch and involved with their children's progress are able to support and enter a true partnership with settings and schools as a child's learning journey develops.

Green: support for learning

With babies and children securely established within our settings and schools, and good communication mechanisms in place, the GREEN LIGHT is set for future learning. Every child has a unique range of abilities and it is through our quality observations of them and our assessments, that we, with our parent's/carer's support, can best meet these needs.

Personal, social and emotional development is about knowing who you are and where you fit in, feeling positive about yourself and developing respect for others. Within our settings and schools we must create situations that allow this to

happen. Hopefully this will support the example already set within the caring home.

We must learn to empathise and support children's emotions and feelings, enabling them to express these. Sometimes this will need our support, often encouraged by our routines and structures of the day, e.g. group or snack times. Such opportunities play a huge part in developing both social and emotional skills.

We want our children to become independent, creative learners, self-motivated, with high self-esteem and a good self-image; to be confident and caring towards others when relating to adults and other children; to think things out and problem solve, sometimes alongside others; to develop the confidence to make choices and articulate their individual needs.

There are many challenges and responsibilities and this demands that we are reflective practitioners in determining how well these are met.

We need to provide a quality environment which will foster the desired attributes.

The Enabling Environment as identified in the EYFS framework (2007) identifies some of the areas which support children's Personal, Social and Emotional Development through the practice which we as practitioners can model.

As practitioners working within our schools and settings:

- Do we provide time and space for our children which allows them to develop their own interests?
- Do we encourage them to embrace differences in ethnicity, religion, language, culture, disabilities, and additional and special educational needs by surrounding them with examples of good role modelling and positive images from our learning and teaching resources?
- Do the adults within the setting empathise with children and support their emotions, which in turn supports their ongoing learning?

Action points

- Share how you as an adult are feeling that day with the children in your care.
- Provide activities which will encourage children to speak and listen to others.
- Promote activities which encourage children to negotiate, problem-solve and think creatively.
- For many or us, experiences of outdoor play as children ourselves create fond and happy memories. For some of today's children such experiences can create a positive disposition to learn and should be encouraged. Within such outdoor environments the freedom and flexibility to select resources, to show curiosity, take risks and be creative can be encouraged. Examples of such practice should be shared through our good communications with parents/carers.
- For all of our children Personal, Social and Emotional Development has the largest part to play in life-long learning, health and well-being.

Summary

For us all, loving and secure relationships play the most important part in our lives. For me and others like me, this started early at home; for the less fortunate our role as a practitioner is significant in bridging the gaps. High-quality personal social and emotional teaching and learning is fundamental to life-long learning. As practitioners we have a tremendous responsibility which is now supported by the EYFS guidance.

Editor's notes

As I read Denise's thought-provoking chapter it brought to mind the words of Margaret Mead:'Never doubt that a small group of thoughtful, committed people can change the world. Indeed, it is the only thing that ever has.'

Denise's chapter really brings home to us how important the social fabric of the home is on influencing each of us. Let's spare a special thought for the many vulnerable children who will pass through our care and who often have some traumatic experiences to overcome as they grow into young adults. It is imperative that we all, within the various services of education and social care, advocate for all these children, including looked-after children, and perhaps utilise some of the questions that Denise raises such as:

- Do we show real interest and interaction with genuine warmth?
- Do we recognise the needs of others as they enter this new environment which may hold for some the challenges of past anxieties?
- Do we allow our children opportunities to negotiate with others, expressing their own individual feelings and emotions?

If we can't answer highly positively to any of these questions we must seriously reassess and amend our practice and perhaps question the strength of our motivation for this area of work.

It is about how we are towards, and with, children that will have a strong influence on how they are emotionally, and how they respond to the rest of the world with which they come into contact. We must create that enabling environment the EYFS promotes so strongly, one that ensures that children have a strong sense of being, belonging and emotional security.

Bibliography and further reading

Barrow, Giles, Bradshaw, Emma and Newton, Trudi. (2001) *Improving Behaviour and Raising Self-esteem in the Classroom*   David Fulton Publishers.

Greenspan, Stanley and Greenspan, Nancy. (1930) *First Feelings: Milestones in the Emotional Development of your Infant and Child* Viking Press.

Kay, Janet. (2004) *Good Practice in the Early Years* Continuum Press.

Mathieson, Kay. (2005) *Social skills in the early years: Supporting Social and Behavioural Learning*. Sage Publications Ltd.

Sharp, Peter (2001) *Nurturing Emotional Literacy: A Practical Guide for Teachers, Parents and Those in the Caring Professions*. David Fulton Publishers.

You've got more than me! 10

Supporting Problem Solving, Reasoning and Numeracy through play in the outdoor environment

Terry Gould

It is important that children experience Problem Solving, Reasoning and Numeracy (PSRN) activities outdoors as well as indoors. Some of these can be done with a large group, while others will be more suitable for individuals and small groups.

Children should be provided with a wide variety of activities outdoors which encourage and allow them to estimate and solve real-life problems. Some will directly focus on mathematical learning and development, while others will draw out the mathematics in a range of ways which are often cross-curricular.

Outdoor learning through play should be an essential part of the young child's life. Practitioners need to ensure that children have access to a wide range of experiences, which involve mathematical learning and development. This should include them developing their thinking skills as well as developing mathematical skills and concepts. Provision outdoors should involve them counting, measuring, calculating, problem solving and exploring shapes in a range of practical and fun ways but on a larger scale than is possible indoors. All the mathematics they can learn indoors, they can also learn outdoors but with more energy, greater freedom and on a larger, much more vibrant scale.

The weather shouldn't be seen as an inhibiting factor but rather as another opportunity of which we should make the most, by providing all-weather clothing. Children can experience making a rain den, perhaps out of large clear or coloured sheets or bubble wrap or shower curtains set up over clothes-horse systems with three or four posts, allowing children to experience the space and size of these structures, both regular and irregular.

When developing the outdoor provision, there should be a focus on the mathematical learning that could take place, and exciting environments created which will engage children's curiosity and nurture the young mathematician inside them. When the environment is carefully created, it is important that practitioners plan and use the many opportunities to talk 'mathematically' with children as they go about their play.

The three aspects of PSRN involve:

1. **Numbers as labels for counting** – learning to know about, and use numbers and counting in play, leading to recognising and using numbers reliably and using numbers to develop mathematical ideas and solve problems.
2. **Calculating** – an awareness of the relationship between numbers and amounts and knowing that numbers can be combined – added together – and can be separated – taking away, and that two or more amounts can be compared.
3. **Shape, space and measures** – through talking about shape and quantities and developing appropriate vocabulary, children use their knowledge to develop ideas and solve mathematical problems.

These aspects should be considered in the context of what the children know already and what they need to learn next so that all aspects are provided for children to engage with, and their learning in all aspects is well developed.

The EYFS advises that practitioners should support children's PSRN development by:

- Providing sufficient time, space and encouragement to discover and use new words, concepts and language through child-initiated play and adult-led activities.
- Providing opportunities indoors and outdoors and exploiting mathematical opportunities and potential within the settings, e.g. routine of the day.
- Developing mathematical understanding appropriately through all early experiences including songs and stories, games and imaginative play.

Practitioners are supported in planning for mathematical development through the EYFS guidance and Dvelopment Matters alongside the Look, Listen and Note.

Additional ideas are given for resources that might be used to support different aspects of development as well as examples of what good practice looks like within settings. This is particularly useful at the planning stage as it gives clear guidance of all stages of development right up to the stage of being secure within the Early Learning Goals. Any resources you use need to involve some outdoor experiences. By enabling children to engage in outdoor learning you will be helping to enrich the curriculum and helping them to make more sense of the world around them. Many aspects of the outdoor environment offer learning opportunities including such things as observing animals, birds, buildings, plants, trees, transport, pathways, the weather and natural materials such as stones, logs, shells, leaves, fruit and vegetables, acorns, conkers, pine cones and more.

Where possible, children should be outdoors in all weathers so that over the year they spend at least half their time in free-flow play and other activities outdoors. This means in practical terms that adults should be planning group/circle time activities and focused adult-led activities outdoors as well as indoors. Ideally, there will be a designated safe and well developed outdoor space for children to learn and develop, but even if there is not, it is still possible, if a little difficult, to make sure they can engage in stimulating activities outdoors, many of which will be directly or indirectly mathematical. The very young child will often simply be interested in collecting items and transporting or storing them in a bag or box – the desire to count them to see how many there are will develop over time. The older child in EYFS will be interested in counting and comparing quantities. The starting point is always what the child knows and can already do, as well as what interests them, which comes down to knowing your children through ongoing observational-based assessments and talking with parents/carers.

Engaging with Mathematics should be a vibrant and exciting experience. Sadly, all too often the reality is that for our children it is dull and boring. The language identified by the Early Learning Goals might be a little less than exciting, but as practitioners we can alter all of that by making PSRN happen in fun ways outdoors, every day and in all weathers. Just as with writing, children need a real and purposeful reason for engaging with numbers, shapes and measures. If we get that right and it's fun and exciting, then we will find those emerging young, confident mathematicians are all around us.

Here are a few tried and tested ideas for activities which will inspire your children to engage with PSRN and have fun at the same time!

Activity 1: Trouble in Big Bear's den

You will need
A picnic blanket
Box or basket of picnic objects
Dice
Bear mask or outfit, whistle

- Set out a picnic blanket in a makeshift tent which is the Big Bear's den.
- Decide who is going to be the bear by rolling the dice – whoever guesses the right number is the bear. Then do the same to choose a picnic party child.
- The bear then hides round the corner, waiting.

- Every one watches as the party child sets up the party picnic, selecting an agreed number of objects (depending on the stages of the children's development in the group).
- Once the picnic party is set up all the children run around outside pretending to play party games. Whilst they do this, the bear sneaks in and steals one or more objects (up to three, dependent on stages of children's development) and takes them away in his bear booty bag.
- The bear then runs away blowing a whistle.
- When the children hear the whistle they run back to try to work out which object/s the bear has taken.
- They count the objects to see how many are missing.
- The one who works out how many are missing and which they are then becomes the next bear and the previous bear then becomes the party child.

Then the whole game starts again.

Activity 2: Double the trouble

You will need:
Bean bags
Two large plastic trugs or baskets
Some chalk
A big score board

- Play this game in pairs.
- Use large plastic trugs and between two to five bean bags each (depending on the stage of development of children in the group). The bean bags represent the children's troubles.
- Mark with chalk where the trug should be and a line from where to throw the bean bags.
- Children gather round and count up to an agreed number. (This is the time the two children have to throw their 'troubles' into the trugs.)
- They can only have one throw per bean bag.
- Once the time is up or when all bean bags have been thrown, the bean bags in each trug are counted and then the two numbers are added together.
- Children take turns, each with a partner, at the task.
- The results from each pair are chalked up on a big board.
- The winner is the pair who score the most.
- The game can be made harder by moving the 'throwing from' line further away!

Then the game starts again.

Activity 3: Big or little three card trick

What you need
Two big balls
Two little balls
A set of cards (see below for text)
Three plastic or cardboard boxes with a ball-sized hole in each
Plastic gutter to roll the balls down
Set of skittles
A teddy bear
Chalk and surface to draw rings on
Magic necklaces

- This game requires a child to choose either two big balls or two little balls, or one of each!
- Once they have chosen, the game is revealed by choosing one of three laminated cards (see below), which one child is allowed to shuffle at the start (you can make more of your own cards to add to these).

Card 1
Roll the ball into a set of three plastic or cardboard boxes down a gutter. Each box is marked 1, 2 or 3. How many can you score? (Big ball will only just fit into the hole.) Highest score is the winner.

Card 2
How many skittles can you knock down? Big balls start from quite a bit further away than the little balls. How many can you knock down? Whoever knocks most down is the winner.

Card 3
Roll the ball so it ends up closest to the teddy bear – teddy is sitting in centre of two chalked rings; inner ring scores three and outer ring one. Whose ball will be the nearest to Teddy? Highest score is the winner.

The winner: Every time a child wins a game they are given a magic necklace. The first to get to (agreed number of necklaces) is the winner.

N.B. If two or more children score the same highest score in a game, all/both are winners.

Then the game starts again.

Activity 4: Fill the bucket (more suitable for nursery/reception stage)

You will need

A water barrel and a selection of pairs of jugs of the same size
Two pieces of clear plastic tubing, 20 or 25mm diameter
Two medium sized funnels
Some gaffer tape
Two large builders' buckets of the same size
Two boards and chalk

- This game is a race between two pairs of children to fill their bucket. Pipes are fasted to a fence etc. using gaffer tape.
- The idea of the game is to fill the buckets in the shortest time and to use the least number of filled jugs (the idea is not to spill too often).
- Score will be five points for the 'quickest fill' team and five points for the least number of filled jugs used by a team.
- One player to tally on the board each time a jug is filled.
- One umpire to watch that no one cheats! (This will be the adult at the start.)

All of these games could start as an adult-led activity for a few times, and then be left for children to try on their own.

1) Each is fun.
2) Each is maths – PSRN.
3) Each involves recording and calculating.
4) Each can be played even in light/medium rain if the children have the right outdoor gear/clothing.

If we think carefully about PSRN in the EYFS, then we will realise that mathematical language is a crucial part of every maths experience. This will be enhanced by:

- experiences, thoughts and ideas
- the environments and present or past events
- exploration of form, space, distance size, colour and texture
- control of movement, awareness of space and of other people.

In just these four activities alone, children will be provided with the opportunity to use enhanced mathematical language and thought processes. Moreover, they will be engaging with:

- social skills
- physical skills

- creative thinking skills
- problem solving skills
- knowledge and understanding of the world
- speaking and listening skills
- writing and mark making skills
- and probably much more.

But for the children, all they will probably think about is that they are having FUN!

Important key ideas that EYFS practitioners need to understand and respond to, through their practice and provision for PSRN:

- Learning goes on when the adult is not involved.
- When the adult is not involved, the learning taking place is not necessarily at a lower level.
- PSRN language is the vehicle of PSRN thinking, and appropriate mathematical vocabulary should be introduced at an early age.
- The main emphasis at the EYFS should be on the spoken, not the written aspect of mathematical recording.
- New PSRN learning needs to build relevantly on previous learning.
- PSRN is about developing visual images.
- Some PSRN experiences and learning are best achieved through child-initiated activity.
- Music and movement are great tools to help children learn about pattern and time.
- PSRN is about encouraging children to represent their ideas in a variety of ways.
- Finger counting is really important.
- There is often too much emphasis on sorting and matching in schools and settings.
- Real PSRN skill is the ability to solve problems.
- We need to support children's PSRN imagination: 'Can you see it in your head?'
- Outdoor experiences need to include the concepts of balance, weight, height, depth, direction, spatial order, shape and size and ideally these will, in many cases, connect and overlap with indoor experiences.
- Physical development outdoors goes hand in hand with intellectual learning, including PSRN.

Editor's notes

We might all recognise that children's mathematical achievement levels leave much to be desired. We need to ensure that we give children the best possible start to their mathematical learning journey, and this starts with PSRN in the EYFS. By ensuring that children see learning in this area as fun, and something they can do, we are helping to build their future success. My challenge to you is to observe your own children and then provide effectively to meet the next steps in their PSRN learning – including outdoor play opportunities. Also, ask yourself a key question: 'How often do I plan my group/circle times and focused activities to take place outdoors, where PSRN provides the planned learning outcomes?' The likely answer will be 'Not enough'.

Bibliography and further reading

Featherstone, Sally (2002) *The Little Book of Maths Activities*. A & C Black: Featherstone Education.

Gould, Terry (2011) *Little Book of Maths Outdoors*. A & C Black: Featherstone Education.

Pound, Linda (2006) *Supporting Mathematical Development in the Early Years*. Open University Press.

Skinner, Carol (2002) 'More than numbers: Children Developing Mathematical Thinking' *Early Education*.

Tucker, Kate. (2002) '*Open the door and gives maths some fresh air*' *Early Years Educator:* Vol 3 No 11 pp14-17.

Tucker, Kate (2010) *Mathematics Through Play in the Early Years*. Sage Publications Ltd.

United, not uniform

11

Establishing and developing an EYFS unit

Terry Gould

No chapter on EYFS units would be complete without trying to define these in some way. EYFS units can exist in a number of differing ways. The following broad definitions attempt to define the nature of the main types of these units.

The three basic models

Model A: The philosophical unit

In this type of unit, the practitioners work closely as a team to plan and deliver a jointly planned curriculum. The learning environments are developed separately but reflect a shared ethos and understanding of how children learn and develop. The children remain in separate nursery and reception classes and do not integrate for any part/parts of the day. Often they share an outdoor area but access this at different times of the day. Sometimes the classes are on different sites.

Model B: The partially integrated unit

In this type of unit, practitioners work closely as a team to plan and deliver a jointly planned curriculum. The learning environment reflects a shared ethos and understanding of how children learn and develop. The children share parts of the learning environment and are integrated for part of the Foundation Stage day. Often they share the outdoor area, sometime being integrated for access to this aspect of the provision.

Model C: The fully integrated unit

In this type of unit the children are fully integrated for the whole of the Foundation Stage period. They share a quality learning environment and their learning is planned for and provided by a team of practitioners who plan and jointly deliver a planned curriculum. Continuous indoor and outdoor provision is provided for either the whole of the sessions or a high proportion of these.

Model C is the favoured model based on my own and colleagues' personal experience over time, and is therefore the model upon which this chapter mainly focuses.

Considerations in developing an EYFS unit

Choosing to develop a Foundation Stage unit is not an excuse to reduce staffing or provision, but rather to invest in improvements in the quality of provision and subsequent outcomes for children. As such, it is likely to cost more rather than less, but should always result in improved outcomes for children's learning and development.

Some of the benefits

The investment in a Foundation Stage unit can have a number of benefits for children including:

- An ability to work at their experiential level rather than at their chronological age. Planning and provision are more responsive to the stages of development and needs of the child.
- Children benefit from practitioners working as part of a team with a broad range of skills and experiences.
- Brothers and/or sisters can be accommodated together. Children are able to benefit from a '2 year' cycle that enhances practitioners' knowledge and understanding of children's needs and formative assessment.
- Outdoor provision (bathrooms, cloakrooms etc.) is more easily accessible to children within the learning environment of the unit.

- Reception age children are able to benefit from an integrated learning-based environment, including continuous access to their entitlement of planned outdoor learning.
- A higher adult/child ratio enables all children, reception and nursery aged, to experience higher quality, child-initiated learning opportunities and focused activities.

- A more effective use of space and a wider range of resources enable the development of a higher level of cooperative play and positive learning dispositions. Additionally, it provides a number of opportunities that can effectively support outcomes for children, including a chance to:
  - rethink provision, including the use of the indoor and outdoor environment
  - establish stronger relationships with parents/carers and their involvement in assessment

  - create a more shared understanding of Foundation Stage provision in all the school team.
- ensure that the EYFS has a higher profile within the school, enabling the practitioners to contribute effectively to the development of school policies and a shared vision. This in practice often involves enrolment of the Foundation Stage coordinator into the senior management team of the school.

The challenges

Many benefits are clearly to be gained, but establishing a unit does provide some challenges that need to be appropriately considered and responded to by the school. These include the challenges of:

- **The environment:** planning and arranging the layout of one learning environment, using a large space, as against at least two separate learning environments.
- **Size of the units:** although units do exist with up to 120 places, a 60-place unit is the model that is most easily manageable.
- **Admissions into the unit:** systems need to be discussed, planned and made flexible.
- **Children's needs:** meeting the needs of a wider range of ages and stages.
- **Balancing the needs** of part-time and full-time children.
- **Staffing ratios:** higher staffing ratios are required. An ideal ratio is one practitioner for every eight to ten children. This should include at least one teacher for every 26/30 children, and be in line with the EYFS statutory guidance.

- **Continuous professional development:** a high quality of practitioner skills and understanding is essential for an effective unit. This needs to be supported through a programme of continuous professional development and opportunities for team building.
- **Observation, assessment and planning:** whole-team observation and assessment feeding into whole-team responsive planning is necessary. Efficient methods of assessment for learning are required.
- **Historical routines:** may need to be discussed and developed, e.g. whole-team planning meetings, routines of the day, structure of the day and timetabling, e.g. attendance at assemblies.
- **Management:** leading a team of practitioners is very demanding and requires skill and experience. The management of the unit needs to be by someone working within the unit, except in exceptional circumstances.

To respond to the challenges and to ensure the benefits are maximised, the school will need to ensure that there is in place:

- an actively supportive senior management team
- an actively supportive governing body with an assigned governor to the EYFS
- a whole-school staff who have a professional understanding
- children, parents/carers who are informed and involved
- an EYFS coordinator working within the EYFS
- whole team observation, assessment and planning systems
- children with continuous access to outdoor learning
- commitment to continuous professional development by senior management and EYFS practitioners
- commitment to quality integrated learning by senior management and EYFS practitioners.

All of the above when implemented must be in line with the principles and commitments for the EYFS as identified in the EYFS guidance documents. However, schools must also take into account the *Key Elements of Effective Practice* (DfES 2005) and *Every Child Matters* (DfES 2006).

These can all be incorporated within the following:

Principle 1: A quality-enabling environment

The EYFS unit will ensure a quality-enabling learning environment where space, time, materials and emotional well-being are planned and organised to give all

EYFS children the opportunity to integrate wherever appropriate, and explore, experiment and make decisions for themselves, enabling them to learn at their developmental level.

Principle 2: A strong parent/carer and school partnership

The EYFS unit will ensure a two-year period where all the Foundation Stage practitioners develop strong and supportive parent/carer partnerships, ensuring an atmosphere within which children have security and confidence.

Principle 3: Effective teamwork

The EYFS unit will ensure that all Early Years Foundation Stage practitioners will operate as a whole team, developing collaborative ways of working, with motivational levels heightened, and ensure that support for professional development and learning from each other is strengthened, empowering an appropriate pedagogical approach in the unit.

Principle 4: Quality first teaching and learning

The EYFS unit will ensure integrated provision which creates broader opportunities for differentiation to meet children's individual learning needs, and which ensures continuity and progression of learning through building on what children already know and can do.

Principle 5: Meaningful school links

The EYFS unit will ensure that it has strong and meaningful links with the rest of the school, based on all staff having a clear understanding of its purpose and value.

Principle 6: Observational-based assessment is the basis for planning

The EYFS unit will ensure that a continuous process of observational-based assessment informs planning over a two year period*. This will ensure continuity of learning for all EYFS children.

* NB: It is recognised that for a number of reasons some children will spend more than two years in an EYFS unit.

The above six guiding principles are essential for the effectiveness of an EYFS unit. Recognition and understanding of how these can be put into practice is essential for all involved in an EYFS unit.

The EYFS leader would do well to consider how these are put into practice under the follow headings:

1. Buildings and systems (linked to the theme: Enabling Environments)
2. The role of the practitioners (linked to the theme: Positive Relationships)
3. Learning and teaching (linked to the theme: Learning and Development)
4. Observation, assessment and planning (linked to the theme: A Unique Child)
5. Organisation and management (linked to all four themes: Enabling Environments, A Unique Child, Positive Relationships and Learning and Development).

NB: It should be recognised that the four themes, in practice, overlap in many areas.

To create an EYFS unit takes a lengthy period for planning and preparation which would ideally be over at least a year. Before making the final decision to begin to develop and then implement an EYFS unit, the senior management team at the school needs to ask itself if this is the best way forward for that particular school and its children.

Some questions to discuss might include the following:

● Has the current team attended EYFS training on integrated learning and the quality enabling learning environment, and are we already implementing these?
● Is the physical environment suitable for a unit?
● Is there a supportive senior management team and governing body?
● How would an EYFS unit benefit our children more than our current provision?

Often as a result, the school identifies issues both for and against the unit, but having the discussion helps to explore both sides of the argument.

Involving the governing body may require someone from the local authority to explain more fully what this means. This can be supported by senior staff at the school who would be involved in the day-to-day management of any unit established.

Once this stage has been met, and presuming there is the will to proceed with the EYFS unit for the perceived benefits it will bring, the next stage would be to widen the consultation process to involve:

- the whole EYFS team
- the whole staff of the school
- the children
- parents/carers
- lunchtime organisers
- the site manager.

If, after this process, the EYFS unit is given the go-ahead, then planning for the unit needs to begin. Ideally, drafting an action plan will ensure that everyone is involved at an appropriate level and that the development is kept on track and on time.

Action plans should appropriately involve:

- parents and carers
- development of the environment
- structure/routine of the day
- teamwork
- links with the rest of the school
- observation and assessment
- planning
- transition
- review and evaluation over time.

There will be a lot of planning and development work, including alteration to the building and systems and this may, for some staff, seem quite challenging. The whole school team will need to constantly bear in mind why the EYFS unit is being developed and, hopefully, will find the second year of the unit being in place, the best year of their teaching career.

Many schools have fed back to me that establishing their EYFS unit is helped by:

- Giving further value to the EYFS as a key stage in its own right.
- Providing protection from inappropriate 'top down' methods.
- Reception age children benefiting from high quality EYFS practice and provision.
- Providing greater opportunity for flexible groupings.
- Giving more status to EYFS practice and practitioners.
- Allowing focused teaching to be within smaller and more meaningful groupings both indoors and outdoors.

- Giving children more flexible space in which to engage in exploration, investigation and play-based learning.
- Parents developing a more meaningful relationship with staff as it was over a two-year period.
- Providing a significant improvement in children's personal, social and emotional skills and their emotional well-being.
- Providing continuous provision for high quality outdoor learning opportunities.
- Ensuring reception stage children received their entitlement to high quality outdoor learning. Schools have also felt that having an EYFS unit made it easier to implement the best from a range of UK good practice guidelines and to reflect the best of provision principles from other parts of the world, as well as those from the EYFS itself. These influences included:
  - *Excellence and Enjoyment*
  - *Every Child Matters*
  - *Key Elements of Effective Practice*
  - Principles and ways of working derived from the pre-schools of Reggio Emilia
  - Principles and ways of working derived from the Forest Schools of Sweden and Denmark
  - Research into well-being and involvement e.g. that of Ferre Laevers (Belgium 1977).

So, for example, it is usually easier in an EYFS unit to:

- provide a broader range of first-hand experiences
- observe all children in meaningful ways in a variety of situations indoor and outdoors
- listen to children – the many languages of children from Reggio
- give time for deep-level learning to take place
- re-visit and recreate experiences
- look at experience from different perspectives – encouraging debate/ discussion/development of thinking skills
- document a child's learning experience
- provide an appropriate environment
- engage in dialogue child/child; adult/child; adult/adult
- provide real and meaningful child-led experiences for all children, particularly those outdoors.

The team leader and manager of the EYFS unit will need specific qualities and skills and status including:

- Sound knowledge of learning and teaching in the EYFS.
- Being a good manager.

- Being able to ensure that robust systems are in place in line with EYFS principles and guidance which provides summary information about all children's progress across all areas of learning and development throughout their time in the EYFS unit.
- Having the skills of leadership, such as vision, energy and commitment.
- Being able to ensure the accuracy of the assessments practitioners make about a child's stage of learning and development.
- Putting into place systems to involve parents/carers in reviews of their child's progress and to support practitioners in delivering this.
- Having respect and status as a member of the senior management team of the school.
- Being appropriately qualified and experienced to effectively manage and lead a team.

The practitioners working with the children in the EYFS unit will, among other things, need to:

- have a sound knowledge of learning and teaching in the EYFS
- be reflective
- be able to work as part of a team
- be passionate about their work with children and parents/carers
- have a high degree of energy and enthusiasm
- have a flexible approach to their work
- be appropriately qualified and experienced.

Self-evaluation of the effectiveness of the units needs to be measured in both qualitative and quantative ways. This will be a key task for the EYFS manager/leader and will need to involve all of the team and the parents/carers and children. Remember that 'self-evaluation starts with celebration.'

Editor's notes

EYFS units are not appropriate for all children and all schools and the decision to develop one should not be taken without a great deal of research and discussion with all parties concerned. It is recommended in this chapter that at least a year is taken to prepare for the establishment of an EYFS unit, to allow time for preparation, training and discussion. This will enable the challenges and benefits to be fully explored. Parents may be anxious about the change, particularly where a unit changes long-standing practice, and this needs to be recognised and responded to. One of the great benefits of a unit should be the continuous access it offers to outdoor learning for all the EYFS children.

Having too large a unit can make it much more difficult to overview and manage. Whoever leads the EYFS unit must work in the unit itself. Both these points are key to the ultimate and ongoing success of the unit. Experience has shown that units which are too large do not self-sustain and can easily fail if the leader or one of the key staff leaves. Ideally, units should not be above 60 places in size, and certainly no larger than 75 places. There are instances where larger-sized units do exist successfully, but these are very much in the minority. So little has been written about EYFS units that the bibliography and further reading will be limited to published articles, and readers should recognise that this book perhaps includes one of the first chapters on EYFS units, so far.

Bibliography and further reading

O'Connor, Anne (2002) 'All about Foundation Units' *Nursery World* Oct 2002 pp 17–28.

Together we can

12

Leading and motivating an EYFS team – the role and responsibilities of the EYFS coordinator

Terry Gould

The EYFS is perhaps the most influential and exciting time in a child's life. It is certainly one many children and their families will remember for many years to come. It's very likely to influence the child's perception of learning throughout their life. Therefore, leading the team that delivers this phase of learning is a huge responsibility, and is both a complex and difficult role. Such a demanding role may be made more complex, depending on the size of the school and how many EYFS practitioners are employed within the team.

Any team needs a manager who is able to effectively and sensitively lead the team, as well as managing the day-to-day challenges. The coordinator should, wherever possible, be a teacher within the EYFS at the school, either in the nursery (FS1) or the reception (FS2), and will, of course, be a qualified and experienced teacher. Where the coordinator teaches in another key stage, this will require a great deal more work and more time spent liaising with the EYFS team. The job will always be challenging, given the pace of new initiatives, but will be made more complex by the size of the school/setting. Leading in a triple entry school could involve supporting at least five other teachers, and up to six or more teaching assistants. This will demand being pro-active and hands-on, with regular meetings and support sessions for the whole team. It will also have implications for ensuring consistency across up to six classes.

Leading a team is a challenging, yet often exhilarating, experience. To be successful, you will need to help each member of your team to develop their own skills, as a practitioner and as a team member. You will need to carefully and purposefully build your team, and to do this will need to understand the recognised four stages teams go through as they develop. You will need an understanding also, of the strategies necessary to keep your team moving forward in the direction of your articulated vision. These stages take different lengths of time to go through depending on the situation and the group.

Stage 1: Emerging/in shock

– Members test one another out.
– Individuals cover up personal limitations.
– Superficial communication feelings are covered up.
– Limited listening to others' concerns takes place as self-interest predominates.
– Apprehension and anxiety exist within a scenario of little sense of group purpose, composition or time span.

Strategies

● Clarify objectives.
● Circulate information.
● Identify roles of people within the team.
● Create a time frame for implementation of work/new initiatives.
● Get to know people as individuals including their interests outside work.

Stage 2: Conflict/defensive retreat

– Personal agendas arise.
– Leadership challenged.
– Commitments and values are tested out.
– Debate takes place over purpose and effectiveness of the group.
– Interests and differences are more clearly addressed.
– Personal strengths and weaknesses are identified.
– Outside help is not wanted or valued.

Strategies

● Deal with interpersonal hostilities.
● Orient to tasks in hand.
● Be sensitive to group needs.
● Involve outsiders for fact-giving information sessions.
● Go public on individual's strengths and weaknesses, workloads and commitments.
● Do not take things personally but objectively.

Stage 3: Establishing norms/acknowledgement

- Inward-looking team examines practices.
- Taking risks and experimenting.
- Leadership and management discussed.
- Finding rules and methods of working.

Strategies

- Offer critical feedback on inputs that block, waste time, or move work forward.
- Focus on who will do what by when.
- Devise and deliver Inset to all staff.
- Practise problem solving activities.
- Develop work routines such as brainstorming ideas, and record on flip chart.

Stage 4: Steady state/adjustment

- More trusting open relationships.
- Outside help welcomed.
- Mutual respect and caring.
- Flexible and manoeuvrable.
- Leadership changes to tackle certain jobs/tasks.

Strategies

- Ongoing review of team's function and effectiveness.
- Allocate group rules and tasks according to demand/need of situations.
- Publicise efforts and achievement.
- Involve outsiders to stimulate or advise.
- Regular social support for team members – meals out, recreational trips or activities.

A few more self evaluation questions:

Leading by example

- Does your enthusiasm encourage others?
- Do you show care and concern for others?
- Do you delegate to others who show enthusiasm, initiative and interest?
- Do you congratulate others for their successes and support others in their disasters?
- Do you demonstrate confidence in others by what you say and do?
- Do you make the extra effort – going out of your way to assist a member of staff?

Delegating

- Do you delegate to staff?
- Do you give staff the authority for successful completion of the task?
- Do you spend time with staff who are undertaking new challenges?

Remember, we are all human and when you give a genuine compliment, to the recipient it is like verbal sunshine!

Responsibilities of the EYFS coordinator

Some of the recognised ongoing responsibilities of the co-ordinator are as follows:

- To support all the EYFS team in having a thorough knowledge of how young children learn.
- If in a school, oversee the nursery and reception classes or the EYFS unit. (This means taking overall responsibility for everything that goes on!)
- Oversee the transition of children from other settings, pre-schools, playgroups, day nurseries, children's centres, childminders or home to school, and from nursery to reception and from reception to Year 1.
- Liaise and seek information on children from other feeder nurseries/ playgroups/children's centres etc.
- Ensure the guidance for the EYFS is being implemented and that the team are being appropriately monitored and supported in their work.
- Ensure observations and assessments of children are appropriate, thorough, up-to-date, meaningful, show progression and cover all six areas of learning – provide in-house training as necessary.
- Ensure that observational-based data on children's progress is used to spot gaps in children's learning and to identify trends.
- If in a school (but also in settings who have children in their Reception year), ensure EYFS Profiles are completed appropriately, and provide a useful tool for parents and Year 1 staff to track the progress and meet the needs of individual children.
- If in a school (but also in settings which have children in their Reception year), hold in-house moderation meetings each term to ensure accurate and consistent judgements against the EYFS Profile points within the EYFS team as a whole.
- Ensure achievable yet challenging targets are set for each child and are frequently reviewed and updated, based on observational based assessments.
- Liaise with the SENCO in the setting/school and other outside agencies

regarding children with SEN or English as an additional language (EAL) and ensure IEPs and PEPs are kept up-to-date and have appropriate and challenging targets. Where appropriate, lead on the completing of Common Assessment Frameworks (CAFs).

- If appropriate, have overall responsibility for coordinating the home visiting of children due to start in the setting.
- Ensure any children learning EAL are appropriately supported and are making good progress.
- Ensure personal information on children is up-to-date and that data legislation is adhered to.
- Ensure that the EYFS has a high profile throughout the setting/school and that new initiatives are brought to the attention of all staff – you should be giving regular input at team meetings or staff meetings.
- If in a school, represent the EYFS on the leadership team (it is presumed here that the EYFS coordinator is part of this senior leadership team. If not, regular feedback to the leadership team is vital).
- If in a school, support, facilitate and lead regular meetings of the EYFS team. Provide a clear agenda and invite the headteacher and/or deputy headteacher from time to time to these meetings so that they are aware of issues within the EYFS. Take brief minutes and circulate to all who are present and those who are absent. These meetings should be at least fortnightly but ideally weekly.
- Encourage and mentor EYFS staff, including providing induction support for new members of staff.
- Keep abreast of new developments in the EYFS through personal research and attending training courses.
- Support the team in attending training courses and provide in-service training when appropriate.
- If in a school, use your coordinator management release time (if you have it!) to spend time in the EYFS classes speaking to children, observing them at work and interacting with staff and each other.
- Ensure equality of opportunity for all children in the EYFS, regardless of gender, ethnicity and ability.
- Be a trusted, approachable, knowledgeable coordinator who leads by example.
- Write and review the EYFS policy for the setting/school, in consultation with other members of the EYFS team, the leadership team and any linked governor. This policy is where you state the aims and objectives of what you are providing for the children. It needs to be specific to your setting/ school but need not be more than two or three pages of A4. It should be made available to all staff and to parents/carers.

- Contribute to the completion of the Ofsted self-evaluation form.
- Ensure that the final EYFS Profile data to be submitted to the LA is a true and accurate reflection of the cohort's capabilities. Analyse the EYFS Profile data for your school and decide a plan of action for the EYFS as a whole, and for this cohort in particular.
- If in a school (but also in settings who have children in their Reception year), compare your data with the national data. Analyse the EYFS Profile data to identify trends, and use to set targets to improve outcomes in all areas of learning.
- Keep updated on any changes in the Ofsted guidelines and use this to make any appropriate changes to practice and provision.
- Monitor the quality of learning and teaching in the EYFS.
- Lead on the development of appropriate planning and recording systems, ensuring these are manageable, accessible and understood by all.
- Ensure observational-based assessment is accurate and leads into the next steps, through effective short-term planning and enhanced provision.

The EYFS coordinator role has two major facets:

- to manage on a day-to-day, ongoing basis
- to lead the development of good practice.

Both of these require a range of qualities, skills and experience including, most significantly:

- good interpersonal skills
- strong communication skills.

Both aspects are important and distinct, though there is some overlap. Leadership is mainly concerned with:

- creating and securing commitment to a clear vision
- managing change so to improve the settings
- building high performing teams
- inspiring, motivating and influencing
- leading by example and taking responsibility.

Management is mainly concerned with:

- strategic thinking and planning
- people, including performance management; making the best use of the skills of staff; delegation, appraisal and development
- financial and other resources
- communication
- monitoring and evaluating performance and delivering results.

Being an effective leader is crucial to taking existing good practice forward. Here is a quick checklist of what an effective EYFS leader should be able to do:

- Ensure shared understanding and a common purpose across the team.
- Have and articulate a clear, short and longer-term vision, including pedagogy and curriculum experiences and outcomes.
- Encourage strong self-evaluation and reflection within the team.
- Build up a learning community of practitioners where all staff are appropriately developed professionally.
- Encourage and support strong partnerships with parents and the wider community for the benefit of children.
- Directly involve others in the leadership of the EYFS in the school/setting, thus distributing this and ensuring that 'everyone is a leader'.
- Be strongly committed to pro-active professional development and research.
- Effectively monitor and evaluate practice across the EYFS in the school/setting through a range of strategies.
- Be an effective communicator with all stakeholders.
- Have thorough knowledge and understanding of the EYFS guidelines, including the statutory sections.

Here is where you might need to develop more:

- knowledge
- being self aware
- valuing each team member individually
- being determined to succeed
- being positive in the face of adversity
- being able to prioritise effectively
- ensuring that you analyse both qualitative and quantitative data to ensure all children learn in line with their potential
- have an appropriate balance between being a respected figure of authority and a critical friend for your staff.

As an EYFS coordinator you will need to effectively and sensitively manage change.

Here are three key elements which you will need to ensure you present as part of the 'change' package:

1) Present positive pressure as an inescapable element of the package – one that no one will be able to avoid. We (led by you) are all doing it, so no one is left out of the process. We (led by you) want everyone to be a key part of the change, but we will also support each other if times are difficult for any or all of us.

2) Look after, and nurture your staff team during the change. Be aware that some will find change a very difficult thing to cope with and will need to know that you are right there with them and doing it together as a team, with you leading from the front. Try to develop a culture that 'everyone is a leader' in some shape or form, and help him or her to take ownership of the change wherever possible.

3) Working together is something which you, as leader, must emphasise the importance and value of, and ensure that all the staff begin to understand the benefits of a 'we can do anything if we do it together' culture. Try to always have some long range plans in place worked out with the team. Then they will always know there is an unknown in the future. Life is like that, as we are continually changing things to improve what we do. Also, use the ideas of staff, as much as possible, to develop the long-term plans for improvement and to find time to celebrate how well you are doing as a team.

Although the above are separate elements there is overlap between them and they are interlinked.

Editor's notes

Positive and professional team relationships don't just happen – they need to be worked on. An effective EYFS coordinator recognises this and understands about team dynamics. Team building is an investment that takes time and effort, but is always worth it when it is successful. I have seen many successes and failures with team building, in my time. The failures were all as a direct result of poor communication and often due to a lack of genuine care for the team. Communication must embrace a clear message and a clear vision of where the provision is going so that all the team know how they can contribute to this.

Successful teams have a culture of openness and honesty. This doesn't mean there is never any conflict, but it is how this conflict is dealt with, in open and honest ways, that marks out such a team. Good teams need a good, strong leader who manages well – someone who listens to what the team says, responds with wisdom and common sense, treats them all as individuals and believes in them as a team. Finding time as a coordinator to talk and to listen to the team as individuals and as a group is often crucial in building up successful team working.

Making inclusion a reality, 13 not a dream

Ensuring children's entitlement to appropriate support and inclusion

Pat Robinson

'Children should be treated fairly regardless of race, religion or abilities. This applies no matter what they think or say; what type of family they come from; what language(s) they speak; what their parents do; whether they are girls or boys; whether they have a disability or whether they are rich or poor.'
(EYFS Principles into Practice Card 1.2)

Our understanding of what is meant by the term 'inclusion' has broadened to the point where we are no longer concerned simply with children who have special educational or additional needs. Increasingly, the title Special Educational Needs Coordinator is being changed to Inclusion Coordinator as the role widens to support all inclusion needs. The role of the key person, effectively implemented, is paramount in making inclusion happen. We must remember that quality provision and a good learning environment are important for *all* children and these must be the starting points for providing suitable conditions in which every child is nurtured along their learning and development journey.

By looking at the EYFS themes in turn, I will highlight aspects of each that will help to guide everyday practice. In addition to the Principles into Practice cards, more information can be found in the downloadable in-depth PDF files for each commitment. The CD-ROM in the EYFS guidance pack also links to a range of publications such as Early Support documents and the Sure Start Publication *Supporting Families who have Children with Special Needs and Disabilities*.

Every setting must have a named SENCO (details displayed on parent's notice board) who takes responsibility for all aspects of special educational and additional needs within that setting. In schools, there is now a requirement for the SENCO to be a teacher, but whatever type of setting you are in, it is sensible for the SENCO to be an experienced member of staff who is also part of the setting's leadership.

A Unique Child

'Every child is a competent learner from birth who can be resilient, capable, confident and self-assured.'

It is significant that 'A Unique Child' is the first of the EYFS themes, putting considerable emphasis on inclusion, personalised learning and respect for all. The organisation section of the welfare requirements in the EYFS framework makes clear the responsibility of providers in having systems and providing experiences that will meet the needs of all individual children. (See *Statutory Framework for the EYFS*: Organisation). There is a clear duty to 'ensure that every child receives an enjoyable and challenging learning and development experience that is tailored to meet individual needs'.

This theme emphasises the need for knowledge of children's growth and development, and that adults have a clear understanding of their work with all children to respect and value diversity, support all aspects of well-being and protect in a way that enables children to develop resilience.

Promoting inclusion within the theme: A Unique Child

- Use the child development overview card, together with the PDF document for child development, for guidance on the broad phases of development. These will help in identifying and meeting needs of individual children.
- Work with parents to identify learning needs and respond quickly to any area of particular difficulty.
- Parents of children with identified needs should be welcomed into the setting and appropriate transition arrangements tailored to meet the needs of the child. Any other agencies working with the child or family should be contacted and involved in transition and ongoing support for the child. This might include speech and language therapy services, family worker, early support key worker, community paediatric service (paediatrician, community nursery nurse, physiotherapist, child and adolescent mental health practitioner, health visitor and dietician). Other professionals will be able to work with you and give support that will help practitioners learn about conditions or need they have not dealt with previously.
- Consider the use of the Common Assessment Framework where other agencies are involved or where there are concerns about a child. Details can be found on the EYFS CD-ROM.
- Have a clear Behaviour Management Policy that is used consistently with all staff trained and aware of the setting's procedures but able to incorporate more detailed programmes with advice from other professionals.

- Access information about particular needs, conditions or illnesses from other professionals involved, through the Internet, through books including the Early Support information booklets and development journals where available.

Positive Relationships

'Every interaction is based on caring professional relationships and respectful acknowledgement of the feelings of children and their families.'

Caring, respectful and thoughtful attitudes combined with good relationships with parents and families will build a secure foundation where children are able to trust their key person, as well as other practitioners, and so learn effectively. This is so important for all children but especially those who have additional needs, disability or particular medical conditions.

Inclusion within the theme: Positive Relationships

- Practitioners need to show a positive attitude from the start so that parents/carers and the child are reassured and feel comfortable. The ethos of your setting will be clear from the way you welcome, care and provide for all children but especially those with additional needs. Be aware of body language – be careful not to give the wrong signals.
- Value parents as a resource for meeting the needs of children for whom English is an additional language, international new arrivals or refugees. They can help with cultural and religious issues as well as language – but remember they may have come from a traumatic situation and so may value your support and reassurance.
- Give careful consideration to the appointment of the key person. Think about the individual skill and knowledge of practitioners as well as any existing relationships with the family.
- Look ahead to transition (especially if your setting has several transitions within the EYFS age range). Will the key person be able to move with the child through some or all of these stages?
- Time is needed to listen to parents/carers and children themselves. Work closely with them – sometimes, especially in larger settings and schools, a home/school diary is useful for exchanging important information.
- Value and involve other professionals who may be working with the family. Their views, observations and assessments will help to provide a holistic approach to evaluation and planning next steps.

- Visit your local Sure Start Children's Centre to find out what services are available there. Establish relationships with the staff and also with the local advisory or children's centre teacher.
- Support all children in your setting as they develop socially and begin to form friendships, making sure that everyone is listened to and respected. *Buddying* is a strategy that can be used to support children and this may sometimes arise quite naturally out of key group friendships. However, it is important not to allow older children to 'mother' their younger peers or those with additional needs.

Enabling Environments

'The environment plays a key role in supporting and extending children's development and learning.'

A quality learning environment is really important when providing for children who have any type of additional or different need. All children require access to good indoor, outdoor and emotional environments where they can explore, learn and be challenged in safety. However, for some children, forms of intervention may be needed. Where these are additional to or different from what is usually provided the term 'Early Years Action', from the Code of Practice, is used.

Inclusion within the theme: Enabling Environments

- Where necessary make any reasonable adjustments to your setting, including your organisation (in line with the requirements of the Disability Discrimination Act 1995 – amended in 2001).
- Check that your play equipment, books and displays promote positive images of children who have special needs or disabilities.
- Parents/carers, other professionals and all staff who have contact with the child should be involved in some way in the observation, assessment and planning process. (That is, anyone who works with the child during their time in the setting – this could include lunchtime organisers, teachers who provide cover, after school club staff etc.)
- Good observation and accurate assessment are key to planning the next steps in learning or possible lines of direction (PLODS). Match strengths or a child's interests with areas that need development to maximise learning.
- Provide a language friendly/communication friendly environment that is rich in pictures and print and where practitioners use descriptive commentary and careful questioning to promote language and thinking skills. (See the Early Years IDP for ideas and guidance.)

- Why not use sign language in your setting? Baby signing is popular with parents and settings while older children love to sign simple everyday words and songs.
- Provide for cultural diversity through displays and learning based on the cultures reflected within your setting. Include use of home languages through print and the spoken word.
- Use a variety of visual support, including a visual timetable for all children together with photographs, choice boards and personal schedules where necessary for individual children.

- Establish a quiet area in your provision where children can go to relax, cool off or just withdraw from the busyness of the setting. Make sure this is a calm, low arousal area with a gentle colour scheme. Examples of this can be as simple as an indoor pop-up tent with cushions inside or some form of den or similar place where children can creep in and rest. (See *A Place To Talk* series by Elizabeth Jarman, Featherstone)

Learning and Development

Children learn through play and exploration. Although specific needs vary, children benefit from time and space in which to play, with opportunities to revisit areas and activities as often as they wish.

Ideas to promote inclusion within this theme:

- Quality adult interactions are vital – knowing when to join in or hold back, when to support or allow the child to persevere unaided.
- Practitioners help language development by modelling (as in descriptive or running commentary) speech at a level suitable for the child.
- Early Support materials are really helpful. Use the appropriate developmental journal (e.g. where you have a child with Down's Syndrome) and work alongside parents/carers to provide a suitable learning programme with achievable goals.
- Break activities down into smaller steps working backwards from the finished task. This is often called 'reverse' or 'backward chaining'. The value of it is that the child has the experience of success while learning new aspects of the skill you are teaching.

Editor's notes

Pat succinctly highlights in this chapter that for all of us who work within the EYFS, our main target is to create inclusive provision. By its very name such provision has the capacity to meet the needs of all children who access the provision. If we fully implement the four themes, their principles and commitments, then we will have created inclusive provision. The role of the adult within this is of such fundamental importance that leaders and managers would do well always to keep that aspect of the provision to the forefront. Meeting training and development needs is critical, and nothing should be allowed to get in the way of this. If we are to improve practice so that it becomes inclusive we need to develop the potential of the practitioners, both in their skills and in their mindset.

Bibliography and further reading

A Place to Learn: Developing a Stimulating Learning Environment (2001) Lewisham Arts & Library Service.

Mathieson, Kay (2005) *Social Skills in the Early Years*. Sage Publications Ltd.

Roffey, Sue (2001) *Special Needs in the Early Years: Collaboration, Communication and Coordination*. David Fulton Publishers.

Supporting Children Learning English as an Additional Language: Guidance for practitioners in the EYFS. (2007) DCSF Primary National Strategy.

Home is where the start is 14

Thinking through the importance of home/setting links, right from the start

Terry Gould

'Parents, carers and the wider family are the main providers of love, care and support for children and young people and therefore have the most significant contribution to make in helping children achieve the five outcomes.' *(Every Child Matters 2005)*

Children begin their life within the family and it is the parents, carers and the wider family who determine the kind of start the child makes in his/her initial encounters with the world. Denise Ellis makes this point well in her earlier chapter.

As children begin to engage with EYFS provision it is therefore key that practitioners plan effectively to engage with parents and carers and their families for the benefit of the child. To do this effectively practitioners need to know about why early parenting is so important to outcomes for the child and how they might approach developing a successful partnership with parents/carers.

The importance of a successful and effective partnership with parents cannot be overstated. Where settings are truly successful in terms of outcomes for children they will have established such a partnership in one form or another with the child's parents/carers.

To be able to develop a partnership with parents/carers, practitioners need to understand some of the key aspects that research tells us about the influence parents can and do have on the children in our care.

These include the following points:

- The style of parenting, more than income, determines a child's behaviour and success at school.
- Children who are consistently criticised and put down are twice as likely to have delayed development of motor and social skills and are three times as likely to be slow in acquiring vocabulary.
- Father involvement, up to at least seven years of age, predicts higher attainment at 20 years.
- Low parental care in childhood is linked to high rates of serious illness in adulthood.
- Positive/quality parental support and intervention at pre-school and primary age are associated with increased achievement and reduced crime and behaviour problems.
- A harsh, authoritarian parenting style is associated with the worst outcomes for the child.

(Adapted from Webster Stratton)

And alongside this what comprises the key elements of good parenting. Good parent/s will:

- value education and ensure their child/ren attend(s) school
- support their child's learning both at home and school
- give their child/ren love and attention and support for their self-esteem
- keep their child/ren safe
- ensure their child's/children's emotional well-being
- provide their child/ren with a healthy lifestyle – including exercise and diet
- teach their child/ren the difference between right and wrong
- model a framework of rules for their child/ren which they will be able to adapt to their own lives as they grow into adult life
- accept their children for what they are and not what they as parent/s want them to be.

From the above it is clear that any relationship with parents needs to involve reassuring and supporting them about the importance of their role as the child's first and most enduring educator. How we approach this can be vital in achieving successful and effective outcomes. It is most important that we make every effort to ensure that all parents feel welcomed and valued; including those parents who are seen as 'hard to reach'. To achieve this, we need to make the messages we give to parents both clear and consistent. To be effective these messages should include/ incorporate the following:

- The establishment of home/setting relationships which involve two-way communication and engagement with parents/carers.
- The clear message that parenting is important, and that parents have not 'failed' if they need support and advice – this will involve the notion that it is a parent's basic entitlement to be provided with information and resources about parenting skills, especially behaviour management. When parents access this information, it must be made clear that they are not perceived as failing parents.
- A shared home/school approach to managing behaviour in the classroom and at home.
- Advice on short and longer workshops/courses which are locally available on parenting skills and open to all parents, with discreet but persistent targeting of parents where there are agreed difficulties/problems
- Enabled access to local family support services for families with more complex problems.

The new Ofsted framework for inspection is based on the five outcomes of *Every Child Matters*, and requires all settings to demonstrate their ability to:

- provide effective preventative work with families and better support for parents/carers through appropriate work with other agencies
- provide quality provision which is understood by parents/carers
- help improve children's achievement, attendance and behaviour
- play a role in supporting effective parenting.

By:

- accurately completing the new self-evaluation framework
- demonstrating how the setting gathers, and responds to, the views of parents/carers
- showing how parents/carers are encouraged to get involved in the work of the setting, including children's learning and development
- making it clear how effective links are made with other services and providers so as to promote the integration of care, education and extended community services.

The EYFS states clearly that practitioners have a key role to play in working with parents to support their young children. This must include identifying learning needs and responding quickly to any concerns or difficulties. Regular information should be provided for parents about activities undertaken by children, for example through learning journeys, wall displays, photographs and examples of children's work.

The EYFS advocates a strong commitment to working closely with children and their families, and sees this as a key underpinning and enabling factor in the learning and development of all children. The key person role, properly put into good effect, supports this required commitment, by encouraging parental

partnership, right from the start. It is recognised that, '*home is where the start is*' and that parents are the first and most enduring influence on their child's learning and development. All parents need to know that they are valued and also that they are welcome. The messages need to be there, loud and clear, not just through words but in practical and active ways. Many children will receive their educare under the EYFS in more than one setting. Attendance patterns will often vary and will include, in some cases, extended care, such as breakfast or after school clubs. Practitioners must ensure that the provision for these children meets their needs and effectively offers continuity and progression through the sharing of relevant information with other settings, and importantly with and through parents/carers.

As children move into new settings or within a setting, then the involvement of parents, including the provision of all relevant information as the child settles, is of key importance to the transition process.

Building up and maintaining a partnership with parents is such an important thing to do that it is enshrined within the statutory guidance within the EYFS. Providers are required to maintain a regular two-way flow of information with parents and between providers, with all staff aware of the need for sensitivity and confidentiality. This should involve ensuring that parents/carers have access to all written records about their child, except in exceptional cases, such as where there are issues surrounding safeguarding, and other cases where data protection laws indicate it is against the best interests of the child.

A few practical ideas to improve partnership with parents include:

- Providing information through leaflets etc. which outline the services available from settings, with times, any costs and names of contact.
- Making sure that senior management, as well as practitioners, are around and visible as much as possible at both the start and the end of the day.
- Building links with the local community and using these to support learning opportunities from visitors into, and visits outside, the setting.
- Providing regular open events which are non-threatening to parents/ carers, and through which they can gain insight into the work of the setting with their children.

- Having specific times and space made available for parents/carers to be able to talk informally. Have available, also, a quiet and more comfortable space/area for parents who would be more at ease with this, or for when parents request it.
- Providing ongoing opportunities with appropriate encouragement for parents/carers to be helpers in the setting.
- Providing a wide range of times and ways for sharing information with parents/carers.
- Finding ways of giving status to the things that children do in the home.
- Planning a regular time each week when key persons can be available to talk with and listen to parents/carers.
- Having policies clearly displayed and encouraging parents/carers to offer their thoughts and advice on these, including ways these might be improved or made clearer to parents/carers.

Editor's notes

As providers, we must be mindful that the more we engage with parents, including listening to them, particularly where it concerns their child, then the more successfully the relationship will develop. Successful working with parents needs a long-term commitment by all the staff team and is very much about the ethos of the setting and how it plans for this as a two-way relationship. Parents have so much to offer, that if we truly care about children then we cannot afford *not* to work in partnership with their parents. The challenge is not to be judgemental, and this can at times be quite difficult. We must be open and honest, and work with all parents and families, objectively and to the best of our abilities, regardless of a familiy's background and circumstances.

Bibliography and further reading

Gould, Terry (1995). *We Need To Talk* Unpublished M.A. Dissertation MMU.

Sallis, J. (1992) 'The Listening School' in Woodhead, M & McGrath, (eds) *A Family School & Society: Exploring Educational Issues.* Hodder & Stoughton.

Webster-Stratton, Carolyn (2006). *The Incredible Years: A Troubleshooting Guide for Parents of Children Aged 3–8.* Umbrella Press.

Wolfendale, S (1992). *Empowering Parents and Teachers: Working for Children.* Continuum International Publishing.

Don't they know how hard it is?

Parenting matters – understanding some of the challenges of being a parent

Dr. Caroline White

'Where's the manual?' wonders the new parent bringing their child home for the first time. Everyone says that being a parent is a huge responsibility but no one tells you what you're actually supposed to do. (DfES 2007b)

Being a parent is hard work! No-one tells you how to do it, you can't do a qualification in it, and your children don't arrive with a manual when they are born. Yet being a parent is possibly the most responsible job anyone can have and potentially one of the most rewarding. No matter how good you are at being a parent, children somehow always find new ways of challenging and testing the limits. So this chapter is an attempt to help parents understand what makes children tick and maximise the rewards of parenthood.

The attention rule

What do you think children want more than anything else in the whole, wide world? That's right… attention! When do you think children want it? Correct again. All of the time. And whose attention do you think they want more than anyone else's? Yes… a parent's attention. We have now established what we like to call the attention rule. This is the most basic principle in understanding children's behaviour. Sometimes children are described as 'attention seeking' as if they have some sort of disease, but in actual fact, it is a child's job to seek attention and this is normal behaviour.

Now, in trying to understand this principle, let's think back to when your child is first born. When they enter into the big world, usually the first thing a baby does is cry. This again is fairly normal and functional, because when a baby cries it is their way of telling you they need something. Seeking and successfully getting attention is a way a baby ensures they get their needs met and this is imperative for survival. In the first few weeks and months of life a baby seeks attention constantly to make sure they are fed, their nappies are changed, they are winded, and of course, that they are loved, by demanding lots of cuddles. This is entirely normal and very important both for a baby's survival and to ensure a secure bond is established between the parent and the child. The relationship between a parent and a child forms the basis for every other relationship in the child's life. A baby needs to know their parent is going to be there and that their needs will be met, consistently and predictably. So basically, for the first six months in a child's life, parents are very much slaves to their baby, by being responsive to their needs.

However, as children get older they develop new skills and ways of understanding and very quickly as toddlers, learn the association between their actions and the actions of others. Imagine a nine month old sitting in their highchair, playing with a toy. When they get bored with it they drop it on the floor. Quite often the parent notices this and kindly picks the toy up, returning it to the baby to play with. The baby becomes disinterested very quickly and drops the toy on the floor again. Within a matter of months, this baby learns that this is a very interesting, exciting game. No longer is the baby disinterested in the toy and casually dropping it without realising it, but they start to intentionally throw the toy as far away from the highchair as possible, knowing full well that the parent will instantly entertain them by chasing after it and returning it to them.

This is a great example of how a child learns that their actions can influence the actions of their parent very quickly. Learning to not do as you are told is a normal part of child development as this is the indication that your child is becoming independent. All these factors contribute to parents starting to feel that they are losing control and that their child is misbehaving. How we respond to these normal developmental changes in children can dictate the pattern of behaviour for many years to come in our children.

Let's take an example to illustrate how a very simple situation can very quickly escalate into a major problem. Imagine your toddler is fast asleep in bed at night and they wake up unexpectedly, crying and distressed. As a warm responsive parent, you go into your child's bedroom and comfort them. You check there is nothing physically wrong with them and you are left to assume that maybe your child has had a nightmare. Despite lots of comforting and cuddles your child refuses to go back to sleep. So because both you and your child are very tired, you decide to take the child your own bed where eventually they fall asleep with you and you both get a good night's sleep. The following night, the same thing happens, with your child waking up again in their own bed crying and distressed. You have learnt that the only way that you can get your child back to sleep is to put them into your bed, so what harm can that do, and so you repeat that behaviour. Within a matter of a week, you have established a bedtime problem, as this pattern of behaviour can very quickly become a habit, with the child waking every night and the exhausted parent knowing the only solution is to place the child in their bed with them in order to get a good night's sleep. Three months down the line, when this is still a problem, you know full well that your child is not even having nightmares; they are just waking up in order to get in bed with you, because that is a nice place to be.

This is a classic example of how problems develop, and so the initial cause of the crying may have been a nightmare, but in actual fact, the long-term established problem is nothing to do with having nightmares, but down to the fact that, as a parent you may be reinforcing this behaviour by giving your child attention for crying.

So now let's return back to the attention rule. A parent's attention is incredibly powerful in shaping a child's behaviour and it does not matter how good you are at giving your child lots of attention, they will always want more of it, because remember, that is normal. So the difficult part about being a parent is knowing when to give your attention and when to withdraw your attention, while at the same time always being responsive and helpful to your child. It is no wonder it is so confusing being a parent!

There has been many years' worth of research to try and help parents understand their children's behaviour. Every parent wants a positive relationship with their child and does their best to establish this. All parents hope their children will not develop behavioural difficulties, but realistically, all children will at times test their parents and this is part of their normal behaviour. Of course, all children are different and some children are more naturally challenging than others. It is therefore helpful for parents to know how to handle any difficult behaviour to avoid this escalating and becoming unmanageable.

There has been lots of research done to identify which strategies are the most helpful to parents in developing a positive relationship with their child and in learning to handle any difficult behaviour. These strategies are often termed as parent training and sometimes this can be perceived by parents in a negative or blaming way. However, given that being a parent is probably the hardest job in the world, it is not surprising that learning some specific techniques would be helpful.

Negative interactions

Before we start thinking about some of these specific strategies or techniques, it is useful for parents to understand not only the reasons why children behave the way they do, but also to understand the reasons that they themselves as parents behave the way they do towards their children. As human beings, our behaviour is affected by the way we think and the way that we feel. This is true for everybody. For example, on a bad day when you are feeling sad or lonely, you are more likely to think negative thoughts, such as, 'My child is always difficult', or 'He has done that on purpose just to wind me up". When we experience these negative thoughts and feelings, we are much more likely to behave in a negative way towards the child. This is very natural and is a part of human nature. However, unfortunately behaving negatively towards your child is likely to cause them to behave in a more negative manner, which only leads you to feel even more sad and possibly angry, leading to further negative thoughts, such as, 'Things are never going to get any better'. This leads to further negative interaction between you and your child.

A helpful way to avoid this kind of interaction is to change the way we think in any given situation. This can have a positive impact on the way we feel and also on the way we behave. Let's imagine you wake up one day and it's a bad day. It's freezing cold because the central heating has broken down, you've just had a huge row with your partner and the washing machine needs fixing. You are trying to get your three children off to school on time and the youngest one spills blackcurrant juice all over the carpet. You can imagine, in this situation you might feel stressed and angry, and as you look at what your child has just done, your immediate thought might be 'You have done that on purpose just to wind me up'. So while feeling angry and thinking that your child has done this on purpose just to wind you up, you might react by shouting and losing your temper. Let's imagine therefore, what might happen if you could try to think differently in this situation. So, instead of thinking, 'You have done that on purpose just to wind me up', you might think alternatively, 'It was just an accident', or, 'Yes, you have done that on purpose but it's just to grab my attention because I have been really busy this morning'. Thinking in this way is likely to help you stay calm in a given situation and to feel less stressed, leading to a more calm approach in dealing with the spilled drink.

This process of challenging your own thoughts and trying to find alternative explanations for your child's behaviour is a difficult thing to do when you are feeling stressed, unhappy or angry, but it can be very useful in helping you to stay calm and to deal with your children more effectively. So, it is often very helpful when your child misbehaves to ask yourself the question, 'Why is my child behaving in this way?' If you think back to the attention rule, it's often to get attention, but sometimes it's also because the misbehaviour is effective in getting them what they want.

For example, a child who wants a biscuit before their dinner and is faced with the parent saying no, may decide to scream and shout and have a temper tantrum or engage the parent in a long-winded discussion or argument. The parent may feel forced to give in and give the child the biscuit just to stop the misbehaviour, but the child learns from this that arguing, shouting and screaming gets you the biscuit in the end. So it's important for parents to understand the function of children's behaviour because this will help them work out what to do about the misbehaviour to stop it.

Of course, the most effective approach to parenting is one of prevention. All parents want a positive relationship with their child, but developing this is not always as easy as it sounds. Investing time with your child is an effective and positive way of building your relationship but this is not always easy given the competing demands of a busy lifestyle. However, the pay-offs of making that investment can be enormous to any parent.

Positive strategies

Thinking back to the attention rule, a child wants attention more than anything else in the world from their parents. So if you can invest just five to ten minutes every single day, building up your 'bank account' of attention with your child, they will actually feel less of a need to seek and demand your attention. You can build up this 'bank account' by playing with your child and spending quality time with them. This means setting aside a special time every day as part of a regular routine with no other distractions, so that you can spend one-to-one time with your child.

Ideally, allowing your child to choose the activity will make the most of this investment. Once the child has chosen their play activity, you can follow your child's lead. What this means, is allowing your child to explore the activity and to lead with their ideas. It's amazing how much creativity and imagination children have when you allow them to do this. Try to avoid making suggestions or taking over the play, and try really hard not to ask too many questions. In fact, just for fun, experiment by trying not to ask any questions at all. You will be amazed at how many questions we bombard children with when we play with them. However, too many questions can interrupt a child's play and thought processes and it actually forces them into making decisions about the play that they never intended to make. So sitting back, following the child's lead and allowing them to make lots of choices, helps them develop their creativity and imagination.

A specific technique called 'descriptive commenting' can be very useful during these activities. This involves the parent describing what the child is doing. So for example, you might make comments like, 'I can see you are pushing the car along the floor', or 'You have got the yellow brick and you are placing it on top of the red brick, that's a really tall tower you're building now'. Most parents feel funny the first few times they try this strategy and might even feel a little bit silly. However, as you describe the activities your child is engaged in, this communicates to them very clearly that you are watching exactly what they are doing and that they have your undivided, 100 per cent attention. And you already know what children want more than anything else in the whole wide world! Descriptive commenting can help children stay on task for longer, it helps their creativity, imagination and language development. It's also a great way to help you build up your bank account of attention with your child.

Most parents know that praising their child is important. It builds children's self-esteem and confidence and makes them feel good. Remember, your child wants your attention more than anything and praise is a positive and powerful way of giving your child attention for appropriate behaviour. If your child knows which behaviours get your attention they will do more of those behaviours. If you tell your child off every time they put their feet on the sofa they will do more of that behaviour! Giving attention to a child reinforces that behaviour and makes them want to do more of it. Therefore, it's far more helpful to not give attention to safe behaviours you don't want to encourage and to give lots of positive attention to behaviours you do want to see more of. So, in the previous example it's far more effective to praise your child for keeping their feet on the floor than to shout at them for putting their feet on the sofa.

However, this is not as easy as it first seems, as we don't tend to notice when children behave appropriately and are much more likely to notice when our child misbehaves. Therefore, we have to work hard at 'catching' your child's appropriate behaviour! It sometimes helps to imagine that you are wearing rose coloured spectacles which zoom in on positive behaviour to help you spot when your child is doing the things you would like to encourage. Your child might be sitting quietly reading a book or sharing a toy with a sibling. These are the times that parents can give attention to the child, using praise and reinforcing the appropriate behaviour we want to see more of. By topping up your child's bank account of attention, they are more likely to continue to play on their own for longer and less likely to misbehave to get your attention.

Parents sometimes worry that praising their children in this way will make them become dependent on praise but research shows this is just not true. Actually, children who receive more praise need it less, not more. The reason for this is that praise and encouragement helps children to build their confidence and self-esteem. Confident children with good self-esteem need less reassurance and praise and therefore seek it less.

So praise is very important for children and really helpful for parents. To use praise to its maximum benefit we need to consider the most effective way of giving it. Most of us say, 'Thanks for that' when someone does something we appreciate or we might tell a child 'You've been really good today'. But what does that actually mean? A child may have shown many different behaviours in a day, and might not know exactly what was 'good' about what they did. This 'vague' kind of praise is not so effective, as the child is unlikely to repeat the behaviour if they don't know what it was they did that you liked. Therefore, the most effective praise is specific and labelled. For example, telling your child 'Thank you for taking your dirty plates into the kitchen' or 'You've been a really big help to me by putting your toys away' is much more effective as your child clearly knows what behaviours got your attention. They are then much more likely to repeat those behaviours.

Praise is also much more effective when it's given immediately after the behaviour has occurred. Research shows that praise given within five seconds of a behaviour is far more effective than leaving it later than that. That doesn't mean we shouldn't praise if you can't do it straight away but it does mean that immediate praise is going to help more quickly.

Children respond so well to specific, labelled praise and it can be very rewarding for parents to see the smile on a child's face when they get it. And remember, as a parent you are the most influential role model for your child. Anything you do, your child will copy. We call this the modelling principle. If you shout a lot, your child will shout. If you swear, your child will swear. If you smack, your child will smack. These tend to all be qualities we don't want to see in children so it's important to try hard not to model them to children. Therefore, if you praise, your child will praise. Parents are often surprised when children start to praise them back but it is so rewarding and helps to build that positive relationship. Children who get lots of praise and quality time with parents are much more likely to behave appropriately.

These positive strategies are the foundation elements of building a positive relationship with your child and are the starting point for managing any difficult behaviour. Giving consequences for negative behaviour without this foundation can just lead to more negative interactions between the parent and the child. Once these foundation strategies are in place children are more likely to respond to rules and boundaries that parents set and to any consequences for misbehaviour.

It's often helpful for parents to have a small number of household rules about the important things that matter to them. These rules should always be stated positively and not become a list of 'don'ts'. Children are more likely to comply if we tell them what's expected of them rather than what we don't want them to do. Therefore, it's more helpful to state a rule such as 'Use a quiet voice when speaking' instead of ' 'Don't shout'. This is also true when we want a child to do something for us. It's far more effective to tell your child 'Please hang your coat up on the hook' instead of 'Don't leave your coat on the floor'.

Communicating with children

The way we communicate with children can have a really big effect on whether or not the child will do as they are told. It's very easy to start ranting at children with vague or unnecessary commands which are ineffective. For example, saying things like 'How many times do I have to tell you' or 'Pack it in' or 'You should know better' or 'What've you done that for' are all unhelpful in getting your child to comply. In these situations, we generally want children to do a specific task and you are much more likely to be successful if you are clear and specific about what you want them to do. For example, 'Go and wash your hands please' or 'Give the remote control to your sister and sit down please' or 'Put your coat on before you go outside' are all clear and specific commands which children are much more likely to respond to.

The other easy trap to fall into is when we 'ask' children to do something when really what we mean to do is 'tell' them to do something. If you ask a child to do something you expect them to do, you are setting yourself up for the option of them saying 'No'. Asking rather than telling gives children a choice. For example, 'Will you tidy your toys away now' or 'Can you go and hang your coat up please' both give the child the opportunity to refuse. If we state the request as a command instead the child is much more likely to comply. So 'Tidy your toys away now please' and 'Go and hang your coat up please' are much more likely to be effective in getting your child to comply.

It can also be very helpful to structure your command so that the child knows what is coming next after the command. Children like predictability (how many times have they watched that favourite DVD?) and are therefore more likely to comply when they know what comes next. These commands are called 'When-then' commands and an example would be 'When you have put your pyjamas on then I'll read you a story'. These kinds of commands mean that you can also build in an incentive, like in this example. If the child knows they are going to get a story after putting their pyjamas on, they will be motivated to comply.

Changing the way we give commands is very effective in increasing compliance in children. Of course, there will always be times when your child still doesn't comply. This is when we need to consider the use of consequences. The most effective kinds of consequences are immediate and short term. It is far more effective to take away five pence of a child's pocket money for misbehaviour on ten separate occasions than to take away 50 pence straight away. The reason for this is that the child learns the consequences of their actions ten times instead of one. It also means the child has had ten opportunities to do the appropriate behaviour instead of the misbehaviour. The more opportunities we can give children to get it right, the quicker they will learn the appropriate behaviour.

Of course, you shouldn't use too many consequences or they will not work. If you find yourself taking lots of things away from your child consider turning the situation on its head. It's always more effective to reward your child's positive behaviour than to give a consequence for negative behaviour. For example, rewarding your child for completing homework by letting them watch their favourite film is more effective and more positive than grounding your child for not doing homework. Try not to overuse consequences and have a few ideas ready ahead of time, as you are more likely to give too big a consequence, or one you can't carry through, when you are feeling angry at the point of your child refusing to do something.

Be consistent

You should always be consistent with your limit setting, rules and consequences. It's important for children to know that you mean what you say and will follow it through. If you are inconsistent, it encourages children to keep trying to push the boundaries. Imagine you are trying to open a door and it won't budge. You'd probably push and push and push until you realised it just wasn't going to open. But if the door opened sometimes but not always, there's a good chance you'd still push it next time. However, if the door consistently never opened you'd learn to not even try it. This is what children do with boundaries. They push and push to see if they'll budge but they learn very quickly to give up trying if it doesn't work. But if pushing the boundary works just once… it's always worth trying to push it again the next time.

Once you've set limits with your child, you mean what you say and you're consistent and predictable, children know what to expect from you. When children engage in misbehaviour which is not harmful or dangerous the most effective strategy to use is the ignore technique. Ignoring your child's misbehaviour is not the same as doing nothing. When using the ignore technique you are actively withdrawing your attention from your child. In this way the child learns that misbehaviour no longer gets attention. To be effective, the ignore strategy means not looking, not speaking and not touching your child. It sounds easy but it's actually very difficult to do consistently. Children are very good at working out which buttons to press to get a reaction, so you may need to work on positive thinking while you ignore. It's often helpful to remind yourself 'He'll give up eventually', 'She doesn't mean the nasty things she's saying' or 'He needs to learn this behaviour is not going to get my attention'.

If you've been playing with your child and praising their appropriate behaviour consistently, your child will know which appropriate behaviours to do to get your attention back. This means that they learn very quickly to stop the misbehaviour that is being ignored and to engage in one of these appropriate behaviours instead. This might not happen straight away. In fact ignoring misbehaviour often makes that behaviour worse, in the short term, before it makes it better. For example, if arguing with your parent about getting a biscuit before dinner makes your parent give in and you get the biscuit you expect that to work next time. However, if suddenly they start to ignore you and arguing doesn't work, you might start shouting or screaming. If that doesn't work you might yell louder and call them names. This can be very hard for parents as they worry the child will just not stop. However, if you are consistent and determined, your child will learn to stop the misbehaviour and engage in an appropriate behaviour to get your attention back. As soon as your child starts the appropriate behaviour it's really important to remember to give them specific labelled praise for that behaviour. If you don't praise them for this, they won't know that it was the appropriate behaviour that got your attention back and might not do it again next time.

The ignore strategy can be used for any behaviour which is not harmful or dangerous. This makes up the majority of young children's misbehaviour. For example, the ignore technique can be used for tantrums, arguing, swearing, pulling faces, answering back, tapping, shouting, name calling, pleading etc. For dangerous or destructive behaviours children can be given a 'time out'. With this strategy children are told to go to a boring, safe and quiet place to sit for a few minutes, while being ignored. It's important not to overuse this strategy and for most children a combination of all the other strategies previously discussed are all that's needed.

So remember:

- Build up your bank account of attention by playing with your child one-to-one, with no distractions for ten minutes every day.
- Use descriptive commenting when playing with your child.
- Use specific, labelled praise every time you see your child doing a behaviour you'd like to see more of.
- Be clear and specific with commands when you want your child to do something. And remember to praise them immediately when they comply!
- Stay calm when your child misbehaves and try to understand the behaviour.
- Be consistent and follow through with consequences.
- Make consequences for misbehaviour short term and immediate.
- Use the ignore technique for behaviour which is not harmful or dangerous. And remember to praise them immediately for the next appropriate behaviour they do.

Editor's notes

To work effectively with parents, practitioners need to reflect upon and begin to understand the difficult role it can often be as a parent. This chapter reflects the Webster Stratton approach to supporting parenting and as such, is aimed at being useful both to parents and also for practitioners who for large parts of the week take over the role of caring for children in 'loco parentis'.

Practitioners will often feel some of the same emotional and physical challenges as parents when children push the boundaries at the setting e.g. when children are having difficulty in behaving appropriately. Making time to work with parents to support them in their role as a parent, without being judgemental, is often one the most important things we can do to support them in their role.

Having watched and participated in some of Caroline's fabulous training, I can verify that this chapter is just like her training in that it gives great insight into how a parent might survive and take back control, when times get tough, as the boundaries are tested and stretched, sometimes to the limit. We all need some of that insight if we are to work effectively.

Bibliography and further reading

Webster-Stratton, Carolyn (2006) *The Incredible Years: A Troubleshooting Guide for Parents of Children Aged 3–8*. Umbrella Press.

Parents matter 16

Valuing the unique role of parents and supporting them as partners within the framework of the EYFS

Sheron Kantor

Supporting parents as partners within the EYFS

Defining the term 'parents'

Studies show that the term 'family' cannot be used to describe a homogenous group. In a climate that is ever changing and adapting to a range of factors and influences such as sexual preferences, economic status, or social pressures, there is little surprise that families are so diverse. 'Children may live with one or both parents, with other relatives or carers, with same sex parents, or in an extended family.' (DCSF 2007: Practice in Principle Card 2.2.) Likewise, it would be impossible to expect a 'one size fits all' description of a parent. My understanding of the term parents and the stance taken in this chapter has been inspired by the Parents, Early Years and Learning model (2006), which defines parents as:

> 'Mothers, fathers as well as any member of the extended family, foster carer or other person, male or female who has the responsibility of caring for a child [with] direct impact on that child's learning and development.'
>
> *(PEAL, 2006)*

What does 'parents as partners' mean?

The era when signs such as 'No Parents Beyond This Point' hung above the school gate, discouraging parental involvement, have long disappeared (Wolfendale 1992). Practitioners now have a statutory obligation to move forward from regarding work with parents as being about specific programmes to compensate for limitations of the home. The current expectation is that parents will not only actively participate in their child's education, but moreover, that practitioners are actively encouraged to work as equal partners with parents to fulfil shared interests and responsibility for every child's development and learning (Draper and Duffy 2001, Nutbrown 2006). This shifting climate has also influenced parents' views of their relationship with settings. Reports such as *Every Parent Matters* reveal that most parents believe that responsibility for their child's education is shared between parents and school (DfES 2007).

How have practitioners previously worked with parents?

Arguably, previous government legislation and guidance outlined in the Foundation Stage Curriculum (QCA 2000) and the Birth to Three Framework (DfES and Sure Start 2002) left room for practitioners to interpret how they chose to work with parents. These variations fell into the following categories:

Parental informing: The setting that adopted this approach focused on having a range of systems in place to informally or formally update parents (usually at the beginning and the end of the academic year), about their child's progress and the setting's daily/termly events. Parents were provided with an overview of the planning and the teaching strategies that the children's setting employed to support the children's learning. Emphasis was placed on informing parents about the setting's expectation of children's learning.

Parental involvement: In contrast to the parental informing model, here the setting attempted to involve parents in the setting's activities and to teach parents a range of skills to reinforce activities taught in the setting. With this model (similar to parental informing model) the aspirations and agenda of the parents was secondary to the settings. The emphasis here (unlike the parental informing model) was on what the parents could do to support the setting rather than equal partnership or shared goals.

Parental engagement: In comparison to the parental involvement model, the parental engagement approach implied that parents and families worked together sharing their expertise and knowledge of children. The emphasis was on mutual commitment and shared agendas that were mutually beneficial to the setting and parent. The setting offered a wide range of opportunities for parents to engage in the setting's day-to-day practice. This varied from actively seeking and responding to parent voice, to collaborative policy-writing.

Parents as partners: Parental engagement has often been used interchangeably with the term partnership and the contemporary phrase 'parents as partners'. While engagement does encompass the key messages outlined in the EYFS (DCSF 2007), I particularly favour the term partner, as it clearly defines the status of the parents. It not only emphasises the mutual cooperation and responsibility of both parties, but also stresses that partnership is not just a policy to be imposed on parents. Rather, that parents consent and make an informed decision to work together with the setting, to meet the needs of every child within the setting.

Parents as partners: key messages

We are all fully aware that the key messages; principles and statutory requirements underpinning parents as partners are not new. The EYFS (DCSF 2007) simply endorses the effective practice outlined in the Birth to Three Framework (DfES and Sure Start 2002) and the Foundation Stage Curriculum (QCA 2000). Nevertheless, I believe that the new framework has created an excellent opportunity to raise the profile of partnership with parents.
We now have one seamless document that ensures that the principles for effective partnership with parents and statutory requirements are accessible to all. Practitioners can now refer to the positive relationship section of the poster, Principle into Practice card 2.2, in addition to accessing research relating to parents as parents via the CD-ROM and web links. This, in my opinion, no longer leaves room for settings to misinterpret the way they could work with parents. The minimum standards are now very explicit for every practitioner working with children up to the age of five.

> 'All settings should develop the most effective partnerships with parents in order to enhance the learning and development of the children with whom they work.' *DfES (2007)*

The EYFS highlights three broad themes for effective parents as partners practice, namely respecting diversity, effective communication and learning together (DfES 2007a). The messages have been briefly summarised here:

Respecting diversity

Involves creating an inclusive environment that values, respects and celebrates the diverse cultural, ethnic and social groups of every family in their setting and the wider community.

Effective communication

Involves establishing a genuine, warm and welcoming setting that prioritises strong and effective communication through a variety of channels. Information, expertise and knowledge flows freely and consistently between parents and practitioners.

Learning together

Involves striving to create a culture where parents and practitioners learn together, complement each other's expertise in order to facilitate children's learning, development and well-being.

What are the benefits of effective parents as partners practice?

Early years' research is replete with evidence of the mutual benefit that children, parents and practitioners profit from positive partnerships.

Benefits for the child

The child should always be at the heart of everything we do, with adults working together ultimately to maximise the benefits for young children.

Research such as Desforges (2003) is only one example that highlights: 'Parental involvement in the form of 'at-home good parenting' has a significant positive effect on children's achievement and adjustment, even after all other factors shaping attainment have been taken out of the equation.' Desforges (2003)

The EYFS also endorses a wealth of research demonstrating how effective parent partnership makes a significant impact on a child's academic achievement, attainment, and lifelong skills (DCSF 2007). However, we should never underestimate or devalue the impact that effective parents as partners play in other aspects of a child's life. For example, as parents and practitioner share consistent messages, continuity of care and common priorities for the child, the impact on the five *Every Child Matters* outcomes (DfES 2003) e.g. emotional health, well-being and being safe is also dramatically influenced (inevitably also, positive contributions to the wider community and economic well-being.).

Benefits for the adults

The advantages for practitioners and parents taking part in positive partnership have also been well documented. Practitioners gain a deeper understanding of how to support the children they are working with. Likewise, parents welcome the support that professional knowledge and skills adds to their own (Buckley 2003; Draper and Duffy 2001).

How can we establish effective practice in relation to parents as partners?

The *Every Child Matters* (DfES 2003) proposal for change set out to improve the information, advice and encouragement that universal services (such as health and education) give to parents, in order to help them support their children's development. In spite of this, reports have shown that parents prefer to rely on informal networks of friends and families to voice their concerns or seek advice about their child's learning and developmental needs (National Literacy Trust

2005). The challenge is for professionals to readdress this balance and to find ways to empower and enable parents to engage in their child's learning through a participative, respectful and meaningful approach (Nutbrown and Hannon 2003).

Part of my role, as an early years consultant working in a local authority, involves building practitioners' capacity to develop positive relationships with parents as partners. Over the years, I have encountered a significant number of practitioners who have had very limited initial teacher training on how to develop successful parent partnerships. This was very true of my own professional training experience, despite having over 14 years' professional working experience with parents. Most of the knowledge I gained was learned through trial and error. I often had to draw on advice from colleagues or familiarise myself with current research. However, it was only recently, after becoming a mother for the first time, that I fully began to appreciate the principle of parents as partners, through the eyes of a parent. I have found the combination of practical tips and solutions gathered through my professional journey, as well as the opportunity to reflect on my own successful relationships with a range of childcare providers, extremely useful when putting the parents as partners principles in to practice.

Putting the parents as partners principles into practice

Respecting diversity

The EYFS places great emphasis on the unique ability, experiences, diversity, developmental journey and entitlement of every child. We are encouraged to adopt a holistic view, where we regard every child's ethnicity, cultural or social make-up, as unique factors that contribute to the varying aspects of their development (DCSF 2007). Conversely, the aim should also be to value every parent we work with as unique. The implication is that we move beyond completing gradual admission booklets that only provide overviews of each set of parents' details, or act as formal introductions to the family make-up e.g. name, contact details, marital status, ethnicity etc. Instead, we should strive to build positive relationships and partnership by:

1. Being transparent – making it clear to parents why their engagement is crucial to them, their child and the setting
2. Respecting and valuing every parent
3. Creating a welcoming environment for all.

   'Being transparent – make it clear to parents why their involvement is crucial to their child and the setting.
   In true partnership, parents understand and contribute to the policies in the setting.' *DCSF (2007): Parents as Partners card 2.2*

1. Being transparent

Settings are more likely to be successful at building partnership with parents when they have a clear and coherent 'parents as partners' policy that is systematically implemented and regularly reviewed and updated. This policy should inform parents about the reason and benefits of their active partnership.

A parents as partners' policy should make explicit reference to the statutory requirements outlined in the EYFS (DCSF 2007). It should inform all the stakeholders how the setting has embraced these requirements practically on a day-to-day basis. Browne (2001) suggests in order to do this successfully the whole team needs a shared ethos. A shared understanding can only be achieved once the whole team has a clear understanding of the role of parents within the setting and beyond. Each team member should be able to share as frankly as possible their views, opinion, expectations and misconceptions about parents as partners. The team should be able to openly discuss the advantages and the challenges this brings, in addition to the level of resources, time, effort and commitment that this way of working involves. The outcome from this team discussion should be the precursor to writing a setting's policy.

The policy needs be very clear about what roles the setting and parents play in the partnership. As a new mother, I fully appreciate that parents want to avoid being placed in a position where they cannot meet the amount of demands and commitment required of them. I want to know, as early as possible, the setting's expectations for my engagement, with clear opportunities to share my own expectations, aspirations and apprehensions. I would also like to have a clear understanding how the setting is going to work collaboratively with me to support my child while they are with them, and at home with me.

> **Top tip...**
>
> Try displaying key quotes from research and statistical evidence on the parents' noticeboard or newsletters to raise parental awareness.

2. Respecting and valuing every parent

According to the Effective Provision of Pre-School Education (EPPE) findings 'what parents do is more important that who they are' (Slyva et.al. 2003). This research has been a catalyst in enabling practitioners to recognise how important it is to empower parents to become confident in supporting their child's learning and development at home. However, we should also bear in mind research that indicates that children raised by parents with multiple 'high risk' factors such as a parental age, socio- economic status, education background, qualifications, and housing are more likely to be at an educational and social 'disadvantage' compared to their peers (Smith 2003). It is therefore extremely important for practitioners to become aware of the factors that are likely to affect the parents they work with, and to see these factors as potential barriers to parent engagement.

Top tips...

In my experience, the following steps are highly effective in helping to eliminate potential barriers to engagement:

- Firstly, increase your own professional knowledge surrounding the current research and national priorities related to parents as partners in the early years.
- Secondly, find out what key issues parents in your community/district are likely to face. Get to grips with your local authority's Child Care Plan, by liaising with other agencies in your wider community. This will enable you to identify the priorities for families in your catchment area, e.g. economic well-being, health-related issues. By identifying the general issues and reflecting on the general needs of the families in your setting, practitioners are better equipped to recognise the factors which are likely to stop your parents engaging in their child's learning e.g. long working hours, negative experience of their own schooling.
- Once factors are identified, the next step is working with parents to find solutions, e.g. offering parent workshops/parents' meetings etc. at times that accommodate the majority of your parents' needs e.g. weekends, late evenings. If there is a need to support parents with their own skills, liaise with Adult Education Services to offer family literacy or family ICT classes.

Practitioners are trained to become experts in assessing each child's individual needs. They continually observe and identify where each child is on their unique developmental journey. They then respond sensitively and appropriately. There is a need for practitioners to apply these skills to assess where each parent is on the challenging journey of parenthood (e.g. experience, confidence) in order to offer appropriate support.

> 'Where's the manual?' wonders the new parent bringing their child home for the first time. Everyone says that being a parent is a huge responsibility but no one tells you what you're actually supposed to do. *(DfES 2007)*

This insightful quote in the recent parents' guide, *Every Parent Matters – helping you help your child* (DfES 2007) highlights the significant responsibility and the enormous task that every parent faces when learning how to support their child's development. Practitioners need to be very sensitive to the unique experiences, support or the amount of information parents require about their child's learning development. The role of the key person is crucial here. The positive relationship between a sensitive key person, each child and their family enables the setting to appropriately respond to the parents' ever changing needs.

Therefore, the role of the key person is crucial in helping parents to understand general child development, as well as in helping parents to support their own child at different stages of development.

Top tips...

- During gradual admission, create opportunities for new parents to support each other by establishing informal network groups.
- Loan DVDs, books, or liaise with a health provider to organise workshops related to different development stages e.g. taming toddler tantrums, the reluctant eater etc.
- Signpost parents to events or activities in their wider community that are designed to improve quality family times e.g. cultural and creative sessions run by art galleries and museums.
- Promote events designed to improve the quality of parents' lives e.g. events organised by Sure Start such as cookery workshops, exercise classes, massage sessions, 'Parent Survival' courses.
- Host events that are designed to encourage parents to develop ways to become part of a workforce. e.g. lead by Connexions or Adult Education services.

3. Creating a welcoming environment for all

This can mean the physical environment, the attitude of the staff within the setting and the way in which important issues are dealt with. One of the most significant moments is the first time a parent and child enter the setting. The old cliché 'first impressions count' truly applies here. Parents make their first judgement about you and your setting based on how welcome you made them feel. This judgement fluctuates, depending on what you continue to say and do but, ultimately by how you continuously make them and their child feel. It is therefore true to say that every day a parent enters and leaves your setting, they establish and reconfirm a new theory about your setting.

Settings have a statutory requirement to create an inclusive environment, accessible to all, along with actively seeking to include, respect, celebrate and value the diversity of every child and family with the setting and beyond. In order to successfully create a welcoming environment, practitioners need to move beyond

Time to reflect...

Having an 'open door' policy is fantastic if it means more that just having an opportunity to talk informally to an adult when dropping a child off or collecting them. This is usually the most inconvenient time of the day for most parents.

Settings that are truly accessible ensure that a key person/secondary key person could be released (with some notice/or for a specific period of time) to talk to parents face to face or over the phone throughout the day.

just displaying a welcome poster that includes several different languages. The settings need to carefully consider how accessible it is to every parent.

Having a whole team approach and a positive attitude towards parents is crucial. Each setting needs to review how their day-to-day practice/routines can make parents feel. Ask yourself, is there anything that your setting does that makes parents feel uncomfortable or worse, threatened? For example, some parents find watching their children sign-in every morning very intimidating, especially if they have sight of other children who appear to be more able than their chid.

One of the Labour government's current drives is towards parents knowing their 'customer rights'. Family Information Services and Ofsted are just two vehicles that are committed to empowering parents to make informed choices.

Ten golden rules of customer service	How to apply the ten golden rules in your early years setting
1. Acknowledge the customer.	Review what systems you have in place to monitor, evaluate and review how friendly and approachable everyone who comes in contact with parents (either directly or indirectly) is.
2. Use a professional and courteous demeanour at all times.	Consider if all staff are courteous and professional with every parent, in every situation and at any time of the day. How do you know?
3. Put yourself in the customer's position.	How do you capture parents' views, feelings, opinions, apprehensions and aspirations?
4. Listen to customers, show that you understand and will do what you can to meet their needs.	What systems do you have in place to keep parents updated, informed and to provide timely feedback?
5. Establish and prioritise each customer's needs in an efficient and friendly manner.	Do parents feel that they can contact you for support or advice after they leave your setting?
6. Offer quality service to the end of the transaction.	How do you record informal discussions? How do you document parents' requests?
7. Accept responsibility, ensure that you keep and fulfil promises.	What systems of accountability do you have in place?
8. Respect each customer, regardless of how you are treated.	What systems do you have in place to address parent and practitioner misconduct?
9. Listen and respond to customers' comments and complaints.	Are systems in place for parents to raise concerns and/or make a confidential complaint?
10. Involve the customer in the solutions.	How do parents contribute, review and comment on the setting's policies?

Make information available about the quality of the provision in terms of a standards rating, children's achievement and even the outcome of complaints. It is therefore critical that the whole team are aware that parents are, in fact, customers accessing your service.

Historically, an understanding of the legal requirements of customer care procedures was the overall responsibility of the manager or headteacher. However, in order to have a consistent ethos in making parents feel welcome, the whole team need to have a clear understanding of the implications of effective customer care policies.

Communication

Strong communication is the bedrock of any good partnership. Effective communication is defined as a two-way flow of information both with words or nonverbal cues, such as a body language, facial expression, tone of voice and gestures. Settings should also be aware of the subtle written messages that can be conveyed in letters, or in notices. Even the way you decorate your room, your choice of resources, posters and the children's work you choose to display, conveys information about the setting's ethos, principles and attitudes to parents.

When communication works well, practitioners and parents feel equally understood, appreciated, valued, respected and able to respond appropriately to each other's contributions and needs. When communication is poor, practitioners only see half a picture of the child. This can often lead to misunderstanding parents' needs and expectations. Furthermore, this can force parents to work in isolation, remaining unaware of their full rights, and being uninformed about necessary choices/decisions they could make for their child and the setting.

Successful parent engagement requires parents and practitioners to effectively share information, collaborate, make decisions, negotiate, plan and evaluate together. It is therefore no surprise that skilful communication is a common core skill and knowledge for early years practitioners (DfES 2003). A brief overview of the core skill for an effective communicator includes:

- knowledge about how communication works
- actively listening, empathising and building open, honest relationships with children and their parents
- summarising, explaining and presenting situations, choices and information in an appropriate way to children and parents
- consultation and negotiation
- an ability to understand when to employ confidentiality and ethical procedures
- ability to signpost parents
- being aware of the importance of self-respect.

The above knowledge and skills are quite sophisticated – practitioners often gain confidence and become strong communicators when they are in a setting that:

- Places high value on effective two-way communication between everyone in the setting, the wider community and beyond. This includes creating time for practitioners to talk to parents. It involves actively seeking and responding to parents' feedback and organising informal events to strengthen relationships.
- Invests time and resources on staff continuous professional development, focusing on the above core skills and knowledge.
- Invests in whole staff communication training strategies, such as how to actively listen and give appropriate feedback. How to share hard messages. Deals with challenge, such as conflict resolution. How to admit if you don't know an answer, or to admit when you are wrong. Finally, how to confidentially convey the setting's policies to parents.
- Has regular team meetings to review current practices and day-to day routines, with the aim of eliminating any hindrances to effective communication e.g. sending letters home with too much jargon.
- Avoids using gender specific phrases, or inviting parents to events at times that exclude a majority of parents.

One of the most significant moments that parents and practitioners have for establishing effective communication, is during the transition/settling in period. This is the perfect opportunity to create a positive relationship between the settings, the key person, and the family. When the key person is introduced to the family, it is vital that the parent/s feel(s) relaxed, thus creating opportunities for them to feel that they can be open and eventually trust the person their child will work with. Parents often feel more comfortable if they have the option of having the first meeting in a place of their choice (e.g. at the parents' home/in the setting/neutral grounds). This relaxed and informal atmosphere creates an excellent opportunity to establish a good working partnership, where information about the child can be exchanged and celebrated. Parents and practitioners can also share their expectations and negotiate how they can continue to support each other. This also provides time for sharing any practical issues such as routines, name of significant adults, both in the family and in the setting, how to raise concerns and to agree the best way to continue communicating.

The EYFS encourages practitioners to communicate with parents regularly and by a variety of channels to cater for the different learning styles of the parents, namely the diverse ways that adults process information. For example, for parents who like to access information by participating, activities such as quizzes and interactive displays work well. Similarly, visual learners tend to prefer written information e.g. letters and newsletters. Parents who prefer auditory information tend to favour parents' meetings where they can ask direct questions and listen to specific answers. In addition to catering for different learning styles, practitioners also need to give consideration to parents' ethnic, cultural and social diversity, literacy and numeracy skills (DCSF 2007). Current research has even indicated that mums and dads access information in different ways. Studies have shown that some men prefer to be communicated via participatory and auditory channels. With this in mind, in order to encourage dads to engage in the setting, you could target a few dads to invite other dads to activity workshops or to participate in interactive quizzes. This is not to say that all dads are the same. We should, at all cost, avoid stereotyping any of our parents. The key is to have a wide range of strategies to successfully engage all parents. I believe the most successful strategy is to keep communication simple, concise, jargon free, relevant, interactive, informative and creative.

Top tips...

Ideas to change traditional forms of communication into a more creative approach.

Conventional format	Creative format
Written letters	A5 flyers with photographs, headings and captions.
	Encourage the children to use a dictaphone to record personal invites to their parents.
	Video a circle time session where the key person explains the upcoming events to the children; play this on an interactive wipe board during collection or drop-off times.
	Simplify parent feedback forms to include tick response boxes and symbols.
Parents' noticeboard	Interactive wipe board with key messages and photographs of children.
	Taking photographs of children during the day and showing them on an interactive photo frame.
	Create setting webpage.
	Visual timetable of events.
	Make an interactive display of ongoing child-initiated projects with photographs, samples of work, child's comments, adult's thoughts and suggest ways that parents can continue ideas at home or add comments.
Newsletter	Record the highlights of events in the setting through a pod cast. Create a pictorial calendar using photographs and quotes to advertise forthcoming events.
Updating children's progress	Provide regular open days, being conscious of the best available time to talk to parents and try to be flexible, with early morning meetings, at weekends etc.
	Provide the option of having a parent's conference over the phone.
	Send photographs and captions of children's progress home on DVD.
	Signpost parents to websites/information books and other agencies to answer any further questions, address their concerns or further their enquiries.
A letter to invite parents to events	Send a text to explain the event and a reminder text prior to the event.

Learning together

Successful partnership with parents involves moving beyond simply churning out the phrase 'parents are children's first and most enduring educators' (QCA 2000) towards ensuring that every parent's intimate knowledge of their child (such as a child's likes and dislikes) positively impacts on the day-to-day practice of the setting. It requires practitioners to reflect on their expectations of parents' commitment to their child's learning at home. It also has implications on how practitioners work collaboratively with parents to support children at home, in the wider community and in the setting.

The EYFS encourages practitioners to recognise parents as experts of their own child's learning. It would be naive to say all parents are able or willing to effectively support their child's learning and development (DCSF 2007a). However, research indicates that the majority of parents have a natural drive to see their child succeed. You only have to listen to parents' conversations about their children to realise that parents frequently make unconscious observations about children's progress, knowledge, sense of humour, frustrations etc. Over the years, there has been an increase in the sales of 'baby' books, magazines and parent-friendly websites, indicating that parents are proactive in seeking information to answer their questions and worries about their child's development. Most parents find themselves naturally responding to their child's curiosity, and thirst for learning. The increased sales figures of educational toys also highlight that most parents are committed to supporting their child's learning at home. Practitioners play a significant role in a child's development by adding to the parents' expertise. When parents and practitioners work in true partnership, both parties feel that they are working collaboratively to combine their expertise and are supporting each other to meet the needs of the child both at home and in the setting.

It is the practitioner's duty to find imaginative ways to increase parents' ability to:

1. Recognise their expertise
2. Support and extend their knowledge
3. Create a range of quality home learning experiences.

1. Recognise their expertise

Partnership with parents is most effective when parents feel empowered to see themselves as co-educators in their child's lives. Consequently, practitioners need to ensure that parents' personal insight of their children's development is given a high status within the setting. Once parents begin to realise that their expertise is given equal status to their trained partners, they not only feel confident to participate in their child's learning at home but also feel confident to contribute to the decision making and day-to day practice of the setting.

2. Support and extend parents' knowledge

Parents begin establishing their knowledge about their child, while the child is in the womb. Parents continue to develop their judgments based on what the child does, says, acts etc. They are constantly trying to understand how well their child is developing. Practitioners can help parents to gain a deeper understanding of their own child's progress by helping them to become familiar with typical child developmental stages. When parents are supported in this way they become

Time to reflect...

Are your parents aware that you regard them as their child's first and most enduring educators?

proficient in finding creative ways to support their child's learning. They become efficient in recognising significant milestones, and are more likely to seek ways to further their development at home. This will inevitably lead them to being proactive in supporting practitioners to gain a full picture of their child and how to meet their needs.

Practical ways to further parents' general understanding of their child's development include:

- Having regular meetings with parents to celebrate significant milestones.
- Addressing key child development issues by organising workshops, or market showroom events run by a range of multi-agency provider/s.
- Having interactive displays on child development stages/EYFS Developmental Matters each month.
- Signposting parents to child development websites, network groups or short courses.
- Loaning child development videos/books.
- Creating opportunity to discuss any concerns, either within the setting or with other agencies.

Once procedures are in place to ensure that every parent furthers their knowledge of general child development, practitioners can then create opportunities to support parents in identifying their own child's specific development. A successful way to do this is by encouraging parents to appreciate that their day-to-day observations of their child are important. Parents are more likely to share their observations if they realise the significance of doing so. If parents are informed that their mental notes of their child's interests, successes, frustrations, dispositions and attitudes etc. are vital in the planning for their child's work that we undertake, they are more likely to make an effort to share their observations. Practitioners can become innovative in finding time or different ways to discuss parents' observations, as well as opportunities to feedback exactly what impact their observations have had within the setting.

Top tips...

Parents can be encouraged to capture their observations by:

- Taking photos of children e.g. loan disposable cameras, encourage parents to send mobile phone picture, text messages, take digital photos, share video clips.
- Have some sticky notes available at the door for parents to dictate an observation, or if more confident, to write brief notes.
- Have parents' observations sheets available at the entrance. (Parents can take these away and write notes at their leisure.)
- Have a dictaphone available for parents to make a quick comment about the fun things their child did at home, over the weekend or last night.

3. Create a range of quality home learning experiences

Practitioners are well aware that home learning plays a vital role in furthering children's intellectual, social and emotional development. Practitioners tend to be very keen on parents complementing the activities used in the settings. Emphasis is often placed on parents supporting their children with literacy activities e.g. reading with and to children, drawing or writing for a purpose, developing speaking and listening skills through song and rhyme, in addition to numeracy skills such as playing with numbers and counting. While these skills have been shown to have a significant impact on children's academic achievements, practitioners need to build parents' confidence to take a lead in responding to their own children's interests (Sylva et.al. 2003).

Top tips...

Find imaginative ways to share/discuss parents' observations:

- Ensure that parents are aware of the system you have in place to document your observations. e.g. children's learning journeys/children observation files. Ensure that they are accessible to parents e.g. jargon free, in easy reach for parents to add to, read or take home regularly.
- Display a selection of the photos that parents take throughout the setting, or on an interactive wipe board at the end/start of the day. Add comment/notes on impact, to weekly planning.
- Encourage two-way dialogue with parents on a regular informal (e.g. daily diaries, open door policy) or formal (scheduled updates either on telephone, one to one) basis. Demonstrate where and how everyone's observations have been used as a starting point to update planning, further child's interests, and enhance the provision in the setting.

When parents associate 'everyday acts' with 'learning', they begin to recognise that the time they spend engaging with their child daily such as bath time, feeding times etc. are having great benefits for their child's development (PEAL 2006). Practitioners can play a crucial role in encouraging parents to recognise, praise and appreciate the skills that their child demonstrates during these activities, in addition to offering practical ideas and suggesting new activities for parents to try at home.

Practitioners can also inspire parents to provide a range of first hand experiences that are not readily accessible in the setting. Parents are not restricted by ratios (adult/child), they do not have to complete risk assessment forms and can be very spontaneous in planning events e.g. when and where they take their children. Practitioners can be instrumental in highlighting the benefits of providing a range of first-hand experiences and support parents to connect with their child's learning e.g. being introduced to new vocabulary, and extending children's investigative, creative thinking, personal, social and emotional development. Practitioners play a key role in signposting parents to participate in activities in their wider community and beyond. This has proven to have a positive impact not only on the child, but can also benefit parents' knowledge, experience and confidence.

Practitioners are aware that on different occasions, parents feel under pressure to spend time, (e.g. at the end of a busy day or stressful week) in consolidating or reinforcing activities suggested by the setting. It is important therefore, that parents feel that providing quality first-hand experiences is not an 'extra' requirement, but a natural part of their usual family routines. An excellent solution is to inform parents that they are the most powerful models for their child's learning (Nutbrown and Hannon 2003). When children have the opportunity to see how parents carry out everyday routines e.g. cooking, paying bills, reading the paper, surfing the net etc., children become exposed to a range of real and purposeful activities.

Practitioners can inspire parents to value the different types of role-modelling opportunities that they already provide for their children. When parents are confident that these situations have a positive impact on their child's learning, they can be supported to extend these opportunities further. Parents can be encouraged to deepen their child's questioning skills, sustaining their children's thinking. They are also likely to create or find additional resources for children to role-play different scenarios for themselves. Practitioners can help parents to understand how the skills, feelings, dispositions and attitudes displayed during these activities link across the six areas of learning and Development Matters in the EYFS (DCSF 2007). Armed with this knowledge, parents can feel empowered to share their observations with the setting. If systems are in place to respond sensitively to these observations (e.g. responsive planning), parents are more willing to work in partnership with practitioners, to ensure that their child's interests are reflected in the setting.

Successful partnership with parents also involves finding original ways to exchange observations, resources and activities into the home, in order to complement the learning in the setting. Genuine partnership between settings and parents involves having effective systems for two-way dialogue, where children's observation, next steps or possible lines of directions (PLODS) are discussed, either informally or formally, at regular intervals. The positive impact of this is that practitioners can build upon the experiences/interests/activities/opportunities that parents are doing at home, while parents can reinforce learning that has been noted in the settings, by creating time at home to consolidate setting-based experiences.

Careful thought needs to be given to the sort of activities that are suggested to continue at home, or the kinds of activities that are sent home. Activities need to reflect the interests of the children, be stage-appropriate, and create opportunities for children to consolidate recently observed skills. More importantly, each activity should be practical, have a purpose, and be fun for all children and their families. Further attention is needed to ensure that activities suggested for home learning are inclusive and accessible to all children and parents, in terms of the following:

- **Activities need to be easily understood by all**

Parents are more likely to try the resources sent home when the purpose of the activity is clearly explained or has been previously demonstrated in an interactive 'stay and play' session/parents' workshop. Thought needs to be given to the range of learning styles that both parents and children have, with particular attention to the range of skills that parents may need to access the home-learning materials. This can be resolved by ensuring that the activities are not overly reliant on literacy and numeracy skills, and that instructions are clear to all e.g. translated to meet the diverse languages of the parents. Consideration is needed in finding original ways of ensuring that parents who do not regularly engage in the setting (not yet reached parents or parents who are non-traditional learners) are given every opportunity to take part (see previous sections for a range of ideas).

- **Activities need to allow for flexible time commitment**

Activities are more likely to be continued at home when they can fit in to the family routine, with realistic time frames (e.g. not completed and returned in one evening). Ensure that the instructions for each activity have an option for parents to either play with the resources with their child, or to observe while their child completes the activity independently. Choice should also be provided for parents to choose whether to complete some or all of the activity.

- **Activities need to be creatively resourced**

Where home learning is supported by quality resources, children are more likely to be excited to continue the activity at home. We cannot make the assumption that every child has paper and creative materials to complete activities. We cannot assume that parents have the time to gather or make resources before they begin engaging in the suggested activity. Effective parent partnership ensures that procedures are in place to ensure that every parent engages in regular dialogue with practitioners. This ensures that both sides of the partnership fully understand every child's next developmental steps, as well as the play-based experiences/activities that will support and consolidate the learning.

True partnership means having routines in place to ensure that at regular intervals practitioners can spend time with parents to discuss opportunities that the child has been having in the setting, at home and the new experiences that they could provide. Funding and arrangements should also be in place to encourage parents to become active in requesting or loaning resources from the setting, or the local toy library to support the identified next steps for that child at home. The settings can be proactive in the sharing of resources by making up home-learning bags that are filled with clear instructions, resources, and practical ideas for parents and children to play together in the home or in the wider community.

In conclusion

Parent as partners should not be regarded as a new concept that has recently been introduced by the EYFS (DCSF 2007), but a principle that has always, and will always be, at the heart of good practice. This chapter has drawn on examples of this good practice and the principles that effective settings have strived to adhere to, namely:

- That every child and parent is on a unique journey of development and therefore every partnership should be regarded as unique.
- Genuine partnership involves being transparent, making it clear why parent partnership is crucial to every team member within the setting, the whole family and the child.
- Creating a whole team ethos where every parent feels welcomed, empowered to support their child, and that their views and their opinions will make a positive impact on the day-to-day practice of the setting.
- Practitioners who are skilful in engaging in two-way dialogue, responding to parents and learning from parents' expertise and intimate knowledge of their child.
- Where parents and practitioners work together to create quality, purposeful, first-hand experiences in the setting, at home and in the wider community that not only support children's learning and development but also, more importantly, is fun.

Editor's notes

Sheron's chapter considers carefully how practitioners can become successful partners with parents and puts this in the context of parents being offered a quality service by settings. It has been written as a supportive tool for practitioners working with children aged 0–5. and begins by defining the term parent, which we so often take for granted. A brief overview of the way practitioners have historically worked with parents is explored and the benefit of having parents as effective partners in practice, is shared. The EYFS framework (DCSF 2007), current research and parenting policies are then used to illuminate the principles underpinning parents as partners. The chapter concludes with tried and tested practical tips gleaned from professional experiences, including those learnt theories inspired by becoming a mother for the first time, to discuss how practitioners can respect, value, communicate and learn together, with their parents. Her focus on practical ideas for home-school working are both thought provoking and useful. As a mother of a toddler, she has particularly relevant, first-hand experience and insight into this area.

Bibliography and further reading

Buckley, B (2003) *Children's Communication Skills from Birth to Five Years*. Routledge Taylor and Francis Group

Chang, GL and Wells, G (1988) 'The Literate Potential of Collaborative Talk' in M McClure, T Phillips and A Wilkinson (eds). *Oracy Matters: The Development of Talking and Listening in Education*. Open University Press, pg 97.

Desforges, C and Abouchaar, A (2003) *The Impact of Parental Involvement, Parental Support and Family Education on Pupil Achievement and Adjustment: A Literature Review*. DfES: Research Report 433.

Draper, L and Duffy, B (2009) 'Working With Parents' in Pugh, G. (ed.) (3rd edition) (2001) *Contemporary Issues in the Early Years*. Sage Publications Ltd.

Every Child Matters (2005) DfES.

Fisher, J (2003) *Starting from The Child: Teaching and Learning from 3–8*. Open University Press

Nutbrown, C (2005) *Key Concepts in Early Childhood Education and Care*. Sage Publications Ltd.

Nutbrown, C and Hannon, P (2003) 'Children's Perspectives on Family Literacy: Methodological Issues, Findings and Implications for Practice'. Journal of Early Childhood Literacy 3(2), pp.1–25.

QCA Foundation Stage Profile (2003) QCA/DfEE.

QCA Curriculum Guidance for the Foundation Stage (2000) DfES.

Smith, P, Cowie, H and Blades, M (2009) *Understanding Children's Development (4th edition)*. John Wiley & Sons.

Sylva, K, Melhuish, E, Sammons, P, Siraj-Blatchford, I, Taggart, B and Elliot, K (2003) *The Effective Provision of Pre-school Education (EPPE) Project (1997–2003). Technical Paper Intensive Case Studies of Practice Across the Foundation Stage*. DfES.

The Early Years Foundation Stage: Setting the Standards for Learning, Development and Care for children from birth to five (Revised edition May 2008). DCSF.

Wolfendale, S (1992) *Empowering Parents and Teachers: Working for Children*. Continuum International Publishing.

Here comes the dragon 17

Why young children need to learn about festivals and celebrations

Linda Mort

The beliefs and values of the world's religions and cultures are expressed in many ways, including through festivals and celebrations, such as those relating to rites of passage, the seasons, living things and revered objects. Festivals and celebrations play a highly significant role in the lives of many children worldwide, as part of their developing life in the family, community and wider society. Children often participate in festivals and, in the case of birth celebrations and birthdays, are at their very heart. This nurtures their sense of identity, values and beliefs.

The EYFS values the importance of all children's experiences, including festivals and celebrations, and the role that these play in supporting children's learning and development in every area of learning. Parents and practitioners can support children in beginning to understand the commonalities of human values that are shared by all cultures and religions, as expressed in festivals and celebrations. The EYFS encourages families and providers to help children understand one another's cultures and beliefs in a world that is diverse and vibrant.

The positive values expressed in the following poem by Dorothy Law Nolte, written in 1954, are present in all religions and cultures, and are exemplified in festivals and celebrations the world over.

Children learn what they live

If a child lives with criticism,
 He learns to condemn.
If a child lives with hostility,
 He learns to fight.
If a child lives with ridicule,
 He learns to be shy.
If a child lives with shame,
 He learns to feel guilty.
If a child lives with tolerance,
 He learns to be patient.
If a child lives with encouragement,
 He learns confidence.

If a child lives with praise,
He learns to appreciate.
If a child lives with fairness,
He learns justice.
If a child lives with security,
He learns to have faith.
If a child lives with approval,
He learns to like himself.
If a child lives with acceptance
and friendship, he learns
to find love in the world.

Sensitive and imaginative curricular exploration of festivals and celebrations can nurture children's self-esteem, as well as developing their awareness of, and respect for, the cultures and beliefs of other people.

Helping young children to develop an understanding of religious festivals through the context of family experiences acknowledges and affirms the culture and beliefs of individual children. For example, at festival times, individual practitioners can find out about family customs, such as knowing that a child's mother always allows them to hide the coin in the lucky dumplings at Chinese New Year. Sharing such information helps pictures in books 'come to life' for children, making them meaningful and memorable. Where possible, it is always good to invite visitors into your setting at specific festival times to talk about their experiences of the celebration.

Some tips on organising visitors

- Always lend your visitor the books you will be sharing with the children, before the visit.
- Always ask your visitor to choose a selection of pictures from the book to talk about and to give their 'take' on them.
- Encourage your visitor to recount a memorable family anecdote to help 'personalise' the pictures for your children. Some families may be willing to compile a very simple 'diary' of their festival celebration for you to share with your children, possibly with a few photographs included.
- With permission, photocopy and enlarge some of the photographs for a captioned display, along with both authentic and child-made artefacts. Afterwards, put the photographs in a 'Big Book' for your library area.

Becoming increasingly familiar with festivals and celebrations through the context of family experiences helps young children learn that members of families of all religions (or of none) love one another and that they show this in different ways, for example by caring and sharing, preparing special food and by exchanging gifts. In the context of receiving – and also giving – gifts, children can come to understand that families of all religions (or of none) think about making others happy by taking the time to choose appropriate presents. Another very valuable lesson in this context is that of voluntary service and charitable giving – people thinking about others who, although not in their family circle, might need practical or financial help. This could include visiting elderly people and also giving them harvest foods, giving poor people Zakat-ul-Fitr (money) at Eid-ul-Fitr, and helping children in need through the Children's Society charity which raises money from Christingle services at Christmas.

Through religious festivals, children can learn that families of different religions may pray at home and attend places of worship where they meet other people to pray, to thank their God for everything in the world, and to think about how to be kind to one another. Children can relate to the events told in festival stories and also to the moral of a story, so long as it is explained simply and in terms of feelings that they understand. This might include, for example in the Divali story, how Sita and Lakshman accompanied Rama into the jungle forest, because they did not want him to feel lonely.

Finding out about one another's religious and cultural festivals and celebrations enables children to understand that they can expect others to respect their beliefs and cultures. One way to achieve this is by sending a card made by the children to a child's family who may be celebrating a special event, such as the birth of a baby, a Confirmation, Bar or Bat Mitzvah or a wedding.

A further way to help children to be accepting of others' cultures and beliefs is to plan to include, say, one festival a year that is unfamiliar to your children and possibly to practitioners and teachers, and which is not represented amongst the children in your setting. Puppets can be used to 'answer' the children's questions about the festival. This conveys to the children an open and enquiring attitude to different faiths and will help the children, over time, to treat other people of various religions and cultures with knowledge, respect and without prejudice.

Many festivals are perfectly attuned to children's sense of wonder at the natural world, and their need to sometimes be tranquil. Many stories told at festival time emphasize a reverence for nature, for example the story of the early life of the Buddha at Wesak. Such stories are ideal for giving children opportunities to be 'curious, enthusiastic, engaged and tranquil, so developing a sense of inner-self and peace' (EYFS, Personal, Social and Emotional Development: Sense of Community). Teach children about the Jewish Springtime festival of Tu b'shevat, the New Year for Trees. Ask for the children's own ideas about how to celebrate World Environment Day (June 5th).

Celebrations are ideal for encouraging children, also, to look for, and to talk about kindness in others, and to celebrate one another's achievements. This could be done, for example, at birthdays, Mothers', Fathers' and Grandparents' Day, and also at circle time. Nurture, too, an enjoyment in thinking of simple events which give everyone pleasure, and ways to celebrate them, for example by making up a poem or song about how pleased people are to see the birds come to feed at the bird table.

Ask families from various countries for information about customs in celebrating birthdays and festivals. For example, in Germany, children are given a special birthday candle marked off with lines and numbers. On each birthday, the candle is allowed to burn to the next line. At Christmas in Holland, Sinter Klaas visits children's homes and talks with them about their achievements during the past year, and their plans for the year ahead.

An imaginative approach to helping children experience festivals and celebrations can support their learning in many areas. By explaining to others how

they celebrate a festival or take part in a celebration, a child's self-confidence and self-esteem is developed, and children's awareness of, and respect for, others' beliefs is nurtured. Listening to stories at festival time can help children develop a sense of right and wrong, as they re-tell and re-enact the stories. A sense of the passing of time in relation to festival seasons can be developed, and children can use all their senses when finding out about, and making their own different festival foods, fabrics and artefacts. They can also express their ideas and feelings about festivals and celebrations in a variety of creative ways, including music, dance and role-play. Festivals and celebrations also offer children the opportunity to appreciate and get on with one another. By offering children the opportunity of sharing the joy of others' festivals and celebrations, we can give them a gateway into a world of mutual understanding and shared human values.

As Dorothy Law Nolte's poem says, we must show our children how to find friendship and love in the world. We should let them see and understand that if we give a smile then we are more likely to receive a smile in return. If we want a friend, we have to be a friend. The EYFS can help us to make this a reality for our children. By sharing the experience of familiar – and unfamiliar - festivals and celebrations, in our settings and through our local communities and families, we are helping a new generation to learn that the world is wonderful because we are so diverse.

Editor's notes

Linda's chapter chimes with a nationally renewed focus on learning through festivals and celebrations. In the past, festivals and celebrations have been a somewhat neglected area of the learning and development for children within the early years stage. The implementation of the EYFS has brought about a significant sea-change which has been supported by exciting new resources such as those of Child's Eye Media's award-winning 'A Child's Eye View of Festivals' series of DVDs, accompanied by curriculum-linked digital handbooks of background information and imaginative ideas for EYFS and Key Stage 1, together with festival story posters. These give an engaging child's eye view of eight festivals – Divali, Eid-ul-Fitr, Hanukkah, Chinese New Year, Easter, Vaisakhi, Wesak and Christmas. The DVDs show families celebrating festivals at home, in their community, place of worship and 'at school'. The films really make you and your children feel as if you are 'there', and make festivals uniquely accessible, meaningful and interesting to our youngest children, as well as being an exciting springboard for both child-initiated and adult-led learning.